"Trenchant, iconoclastic, and heartfelt—in short, true."—Rick Moody

At his dying mother's bedside, Bill Henderson promised that he would finally settle down, after years of the single life in New York, and have a family. Following many marital ups and downs and hilarious misadventures, his daughter was born four years later. *Her Father* is a highly personal yet universally familiar account of one man's passage to fatherhood and concurrent spiritual reawakening.

"A brave, warts-and-all memoir."—*Booklist*

"A shivering, quaking memoir of broken faith that needed an earthly miracle . . . the raw truth."—Marvin Bell

"An endearingly simple, straightforward love story." —Edward Hoagland

Her Father

A MEMOIR
BILL HENDERSON

PUSHCART PRESS
WAINSCOTT, NEW YORK

© 2000 Bill Henderson
All rights reserved
ISBN 1-888889-16-0
Published by Pushcart Press
P.O. Box 380
Wainscott, New York 11975
Distributed by
W.W. Norton & Co.

First published in hardcover by
Faber and Faber, Inc.

I should not talk so much about myself if there were anybody else who I knew so well. Unfortunately, I am confined to this theme by the narrowness of my experience. Moreover, I, on my side, require of every writer, first or lastly, a simple and sincere account of his own life, and not merely what he has heard of other men's lives.

Thoreau, *Walden*

Her Father

I

Philadelphia, 1980

1

The Sigh

WEEKS AGO, before they began the morphine, I had told Mom the last and most important thing I wanted her to know. "I'm going to get married again, have a child some day!"

I yelled this into the receiver of a pay phone next to a roaring highway on the east end of Long Island. They had told me she might die that day.

"A baby!" she cried.

"Yes, a baby!" I yelled again, to be sure she remembered what she had heard.

Then I sped to the airport and flew down to Philadelphia to be with her for the end.

But she fought on for weeks.

On the morning of her last day, September 5, 1980, she slept. "Semicomatose," her doctor said.

Her lungs had filled with fluid. The nurses roused her, attached a mouthpiece to her lips and aspirated her lungs, which left her gasping for air, red-faced.

I grabbed the doctor. "I want her *out*."

He understood. He promised to double the morphine dose.

I went to Mom's house that night, left my brother Bob on nightwatch at her bedside. Just before ten P.M., Bob called me: "I think she is dying." When I rushed into the hospital room minutes later, her mouth was open and her lidless eyes half closed. The light overhead shone directly on her face. Her chest, which had been heaving in her struggle for air for almost a month, was finally still.

"Mom, it's me. I'm here, Mom," I said loudly. The nurse had informed me that hearing is the last sense to fail. "I'm here now, Mom!"

I wanted her to know that her elder son was with her when she died, the son who had promised her he would be married again and have children. The son who wrote things on paper—even taking notes at her bedside—who laughed at her minister's sermons, got divorced. That son.

But she was motionless.

The doctor arrived, felt for her pulse, said, "She's gone." They elevated the mattress a few feet, a sign that it now held a corpse.

"Would you like some time with her?" the nurse asked. Bob nodded. We had thirty minutes, she said.

We became curiously practical, packing up her slippers, what little clothing she had brought with her, the photos of Bob's children and the crayon drawings they had made for their sick grandmother.

I became obsessed with her open mouth, frozen in its final gasp. If there were a viewing, I did not want her to be embarrassed by this fishy grimace. And I didn't want the undertaker to break her jaw after it was set in rigor mortis.

I slung a towel under her jaw, shut her mouth with my hands, and tied it over her head. But the towel wouldn't hold her mouth shut. I propped a pillow under her jaw but that didn't work either. I felt her growing colder. I quit with the jaw.

Two guys arrived with a gurney to take her downstairs to the hospital morgue. Bob was struggling with her engagement and wedding rings. They seemed to be stuck on her finger and he was worried they'd be stolen. These rings were terribly important to her. I remembered her cries decades ago when she thought she had lost them.

I lifted her hand to help him and watched it drop. A dead hand. My mother's dead hand. The hand that had caressed me, fed me, washed me. I couldn't comprehend the hand.

Finally we slipped the rings from her finger, looked around the room for a final time, and left.

It was eleven o'clock on a September night, and my brother and I were not prepared with an appropriate ceremony beyond the practicality of tidying up the corpse and calling our sister. We went to a local bar and drank silently.

Next to us, a lady of Mother's age drank too until she was sodden. Bob helped the lady out the door. "A good boy," the lady mumbled as they left. He saw her across the street to her house.

When he returned I asked him for the first time, "What do you think Mom meant with that sigh today?"

"She was probably just mad at you for your note-taking," he said.

I was suddenly furious at him, and at her, for their dismissal of my note-taking.

I did not grieve. I boiled.

The minister's name was Waldermülder—"watermelon," as I had satirized him to Mother, somebody round of form and squishy of mind. She ignored my jibes.

I demanded that this minister give her a funeral that shouted aloud for immortality. No anonymous, packaged service, inoffensive to all, I demanded.

My mother believed that she was "going to heaven to find Daddy" and that "we will all be together again in heaven." To some in her suburban congregation such thoughts were a bit naive, to others embarrassing. But I wanted no shilly-shallying. I wanted a celebration of what she believed.

Dr. Waldermülder did what I ordered. The huge Bryn Mawr Presbyterian Church filled to standing room only with the people Mom had touched in her life. The stones rang with their hymns.

They had come only for love of her. There was no other business or social reason for their being there. Mom did no business, partook in no society hoopla.

The singing broke through my anger at her sigh and set my lips trembling.

The Bible reading was from Proverbs 31. "A good wife, who can find? She is worth far more than rubies. Her husband trusts in her, and she never lacks gain. She brings him good and not harm, all the days of her life. . . . Her children rise and bless her," Waldermülder read.

Bob decided that a hermetically sealed metal box might keep the worms out, but it also might prevent Mom from rising from the dead when Jesus returned. We buried her in a wooden coffin.

In her arms we placed a Bible that I had given her after my father died years ago, an attempt then to convince her that I had at least a sliver of respect for her church.

Her burial dress was selected by my sister, Ruth, who had converted to Judaism when she married. It was a dress they both had loved.

At the gathering in Mom's house after the funeral, a neighbor told me a story from that past summer. The neighbor had apologized to my dying mother for the noise of his grandkids playing in a backyard pool next door. "Oh goodness," said Mom. "They can make all the noise they like. The more kids the better."

That did it for my anger about the notebooks. In tears, I wandered the backyard talking to my dead mom, convinced I was truly talking to her, about the weather, her friends, the family dog, September flowers, the child I would have—joking with her that if I told Watermelon about this conversation he would consider me mad. "Sermons about immortality are one thing, Mom. Talking to the dead quite another!" I laughed to her, a final howling gibe at her minister.

In the months afterward, we three children cleaned out the house she had lived in alone in her final years. As drugs and burglaries had invaded the suburbs, she had installed an alarm system with a red panic button over her bed. She had never used it. Prayer was her protection.

In this house she and Pop had raised their three kids and brought all family problems to God, Jesus, and the Holy Ghost, who shared the house with us as real tenants. This was God's house. Our house, and all of us, were for God.

But after her death all the tenants were gone. God's house was empty and soon sold. A fancy development appeared in the woods behind it. These suburbs had become utterly boring to me, and occasionally I thought of her as just as boring.

Maybe she believed in Jesus, immortality and the rest because she had no imagination. Maybe her constant kindness was just a symptom of her humorlessness.

Was that why she had fallen back and sighed when she caught me taking notes at her deathbed, because she was too dull to understand what I was trying to do with those notes?

She had been dying for twelve years.

First the cancer had appeared in one breast, and after that it had moved to her other breast, and when that was removed, to her bones, and finally it was everywhere. The doctors operated, switched male and female hormones, tried radiation and chemotherapy.

She grew a mustache on male hormones and lost it when they changed to female. Her hair fell out during the chemotherapy and grew back in. Some drugs made her hallucinate. This horrified her. Her mind had always been clear, and more than the pain, the loss of clarity was unbearable.

I lived in New York City, but visited her at least once a month.

Every time I saw her, I reverted to a pubescent boy, bragging of my drinking exploits, hinting about all the women in my single man's bed, satirizing the church where she served as a deacon, mocking her bridge parties, hooting at Lawrence Welk—the only TV program she would watch.

Now and then a girlfriend made the trip from New York with

me and watched this grown man she had been dating become a chuckling, sniveling brat in front of his mother.

I felt it happening, observed myself showing off for Mom. I couldn't help it. And did it anyway.

I sensed in that silent house an overwhelming oppression my father had left us. Dead for over a decade, he seemed to live on there in fear and timidity and paralyzing shyness. For thirty-eight years Mom had been devoted to this man's routines of church and work. For thirty-eight years she had seen him out the door in the morning as he traveled the area to fix low-voltage switch gear, whatever that was, for General Electric Company. She followed him off to church on Sunday morning and again at night for hymn singing.

Every time I walked in her door, I clowned for this sick woman. I danced so that she would look at me, so that her love for her son would be a love for the person I had become. In my perpetual naughtiness, I begged her to pay attention to me.

"That Bill," she'd say to my date and shake her head. "He's just a little boy."

The date would be perplexed at my mother's ignorance of her son and sure that I had gone nuts.

But I was convinced of the sacredness of my craziness. The wrong ideas sent you to hell, Pop had said. Although she didn't believe in hell, Mom would not contradict him. Now I worshiped new right ideas and there was no way this tired, good woman could join me in these ideas.

She could only smile at the fervor of it all.

"Do your best" was her rule. Whenever her children were rewarded for doing their best, she appeared for the occasion. Her motto was a challenge to incredible heights of "best," I imagined.

Pop's motto was a feeble and uncertain "Be good."

One day after Pop died she described him as "a Caspar Milquetoast." It was a quiet, offhand, breakfast table comment. Had I heard her correctly? Did she realize what she had just said? Had she just damned her husband? Was she sure of the reference? Didn't she really mean Casper the Friendly Ghost?

After Pop died the uncles removed his tools and work table from the garage, and Mom offered the garage to me as a shipping room for my small publishing company. There I was at war with the corporate book behemoths who had rejected my first novel (a novel now self-published and on my list).

I took the train down from New York and stuffed books, taped boxes, and applied labels in the garage. Then I piled the boxes in Mom's Buick and drove them to the post office.

One cool spring day, the second edition of my annual small press literary anthology *The Pushcart Prize* had to be shipped to over two hundred B. Dalton and Waldenbooks stores—two or three books per store in each box, plus invoice. The line of empty boxes ran almost the two-hundred-foot length of the driveway.

In *Pushcart Prize II* were two stories by unknowns named John Irving and Tim O'Brien reprinted from *Antaeus* and *Ploughshares*, plus dozens of poems, essays, and stories by other authors, some recognized, most not. All ignored by the behemoths.

I danced as I stuffed my boxes. I danced for my cause, for helping to rescue small presses and small-press authors from oblivion. I danced for striking a blow at greedy publishing conglomerates that had turned publishing into money-grubbing. I danced too because my effort had been recognized, even celebrated.

I danced for my mother's eyes.

She watched me from the living room window, lying in her reclining chair, exhausted by the cancer.

Did she understand that I had done a good thing? That I had tried my best and won a victory for the underdog? That I had returned to Philadelphia in a sort of triumph? Did she see me as anything more than a demented, frantic box-stuffer?

Later she knocked on the window and beckoned me to come inside. A phone call, she told me. Bonnie somebody.

Bonnie lived around the corner from me in New York. Some nights she stayed with me; some nights I rounded the corner and slept with her. Other nights were for sleeping with whoever turned up at the Lion's Head Bar in the Village, or at a party, and felt in the mood.

While Mom sat in her chair by the window, I took the call on the couch.

"I just want you to know I am pregnant and I am having an abortion tomorrow morning," Bonnie said.

"I see," I said, unable to say more in front of Mom.

"It's probably your baby, but there was one other guy one night last month, so I don't know. I will pay for it."

"Can't you wait until I get back and we can talk?"

"No. I've made the appointment."

"OK. But I have to think. I may call you back."

"I just wanted you to know what I am doing," Bonnie said, and hung up.

I went back to my line of boxes.

Maybe Bonnie was right. There was a chance it wasn't my kid. Therefore it was her decision alone, and I was off the hook. But Bonnie and I both knew it was almost certainly my child.

I should stop her. Try to make arrangements for the child's birth. Anything. Or at least protest.

I worried the rest of the afternoon, my mother watching me from the window.

What did books mean to Mom? I wondered, my dance slowing to a plod. She once told me that all the stories had already been written in the Bible. What was the need for more stories?

Other than the Bible, the only book she or Pop read was *I Was a Pagan* by V. S. Kitchen. Pop was addicted to this 1930s tale of a degenerate who converted to follow Jesus. He read it compulsively, almost every night for decades, until his death.

Mom subscribed to Book-of-the-Month Club and Reader's Digest Condensed Book Club, but she never read the selections. They lined up unopened on the shelves bordering the fireplace, where no fire was ever lighted.

As the sun set, I taped and labeled my boxes and carried them to the car. My two hundred boxes of poetry, stories, and essays—my Johnny Appleseed compulsion.

Mom watched.

Through the early years of her cancer treatment, after her left breast was removed, Mom rose weekdays at 6:15, made breakfast for herself and any of her children who happened to be visiting, and then taught math all day at the local high school. Most years the kids voted her their favorite teacher. After school, she coached the cheerleaders, who often visited her at home for cookies and practice in the backyard. Mom coached her girls kindly and seemed oblivious to their half-naked leapings and war cries. To her these were nice girls, and niceness was all Mom required of anybody. Gridiron sex and brutality . . . these were ideas her son brought up at the dinner table to upset her, trying to get her attention with his odd sense of humor.

But she seldom lost her calm. Only once after Pop died did she confess her disappointment in this son who had turned out so different from what she and Pop had planned. "I'm so lonely," she said, putting down her fork, the tears starting. "I know Daddy's in heaven, but I'm down here all alone."

In the weeks just after Pop's death, she began to join me in a small glass of wine with dinner, perhaps to let me know she wasn't such a prude after all. Alcohol was a major sin in Pop's eyes, a joy in mine, a way out of shyness.

Once, in disgust with the pain of her disease, she said "shit," perhaps trying to reach out to me in the profane language that I used now and then.

To Pop, even "heck" was taboo.

I looked at her, appalled. My mother did not use such words and I couldn't imagine why she had done it.

She saw the shock in my eyes and never said "shit" again. Not when the doctor told her that her right breast too would have to be removed; not when they began to find cancer everywhere; not when she became too weak to leave the house for her monthly bridge club meeting, or her deacon's duties at church, or her Meals-on-Wheels visits to shut-ins.

Never in her long final decline, sleeping away her days in the white reclining chair by the window, being carried by my brother to the doctor's office, or to the hospital for painful drains into her chest cavity, she never once complained, and she never said "shit."

When we were all much younger, Mom and her three kids spent long summer days at the beach in Ocean City, New Jersey. We kids built sandcastles and fought play battles on rubber rafts while real battles happened in other countries. Mom chatted with other mothers under her umbrella, coated us with Gaby suntan lotion, fed us copious beach picnics, and read *McCall's* and *Ladies' Home Journal*.

We saw Pop only on weekends. Then, on Sundays, he drove us to a nondenominational one-room church nearby where we heard messages about the advancing communist horde, the certain world conflagration, and the blessed Second Coming of Jesus. When Pop left on Monday morning for Philadelphia and his General Electric job, we went back to the peaceful beach with Mom.

At night she tucked her children in to bed and heard our prayers. As the oldest I had more to say to God than did Bob or Ruth. "Now I lay me down to sleep, I pray the Lord my soul to keep," I'd pray silently to myself. It was quicker silently. "God bless Daddy, Mommy, Bob, Ruth" was followed by a list of "God blesses" that I meant to be inclusive of my entire boy's universe. It would be a sin to leave somebody out, at least somebody important. What if something happened to someone in the night because I forgot to mention their name to God? Silently I prayed with my eyes closed, while the ocean washed a few blocks away and my mother knelt by the bed, waiting for me to finish and say "Amen" out loud.

One night I ranged over all my relatives, Eisenhower and Khrushchev ("May he forsake Communism and turn to Jesus"), my classmates at summer Bible school, all the animals in the woods and on the shore, all the creatures in the ocean, all the bars and saloons ("May they become churches"), Del Ennis, Robin Roberts . . . I was halfway through the Philadelphia Phillies squad when Mom snapped, "You're not praying! You're pretending!"

She stood up and was gone.

"I was too praying!" I shouted, wounded and scared.

She returned and knelt down again at my bedside. "I'm sorry," she said.

I finished my silent list and said "Amen" out loud.

She kissed me goodnight, and left me alone in the dark wondering how she could think I would fake a prayer to God. Did my mother think I was a liar? Who did she think I was?

Many summers later, when I was sixteen, I fell asleep at the summer house of my first girlfriend. The house was miles away from our place. I slept from the exhaustion of working a twelve-hour day as a boardwalk drugstore clerk, not from passion, of which I knew little. Lizzie and I had tried a bit of passion—I had wrestled her pajamas to her knees and she had wrestled them back up many times. Sometime after midnight, she finally said, "Ahhh, okay," and pulled her own bottoms down.

But by then I was too tired to produce much. Since I knew nothing about such matters, had never heard the words *erection* or *impotence*, I slept well and untroubled.

At first light, I woke suddenly. I ran out to the family car, which I'd parked outside Lizzie's house, and hurried home. Too late.

A few blocks down the road, in the early morning dimness, I saw Mom, three miles into a middle-of-the-night march to rescue her son from sin, disease, and a shotgun wedding.

I stopped and picked her up. "We didn't do anything," was all I could manage. The truth.

She stared out the window in fury.

Pop was asleep when we pulled in. I don't think she ever told him about her walk through the night to save me from Lizzie. Pop wouldn't have known what to say about such matters.

"If you don't know what good is, I can't tell you," he'd say if pressed for details.

Mom said only that we should know the difference between right and wrong. If asked, she tried to provide detailed instructions.

About sex, for instance. After the Lizzie incident, she handed me a pamphlet. I read a few pages about conception and dozens about the terrors of gonorrhea and syphilis.

About drinking and smoking, Mom said both were wrong simply because they harmed your body. Pop was Biblical: "Wine is a mocker, strong drink is raging, and whomsoever is deceived thereby is not wise." His dad had been, for a time, an unwise souse.

Mom thought the wars in Korea and Vietnam were terrible but necessary. "We have to help out people the best we can," she said.

Martin Luther King, Jr. was a troublemaker and didn't deserve the Nobel Prize, according to Mom. Interracial marriage was wrong only because of the ostracism that biracial children would suffer. But prejudice against anybody was also wrong and she knew of nobody around her who had such prejudices.

In Mom's calm house arguments were rare. We were quiet people. Our hallelujahs were unshouted and unsung. There was little laughter beyond the shouts of children at play. And that was all our parents required.

A daily dose of passion ripped from the radio every morning in the voice of evangelist Carl MacIntire and his "Twentieth Century Reformation Hour," a breakfast show. He harangued that Jesus would soon incinerate the Reds and all sinners and elevate God's children (us) to heaven with him for eternity.

Pop nodded his head, spooned his cereal, and listened carefully, although MacIntire said the same thing every morning.

Mom ignored the racket. She cheerily served up our hot oatmeal and cod liver oil and orange juice and readied us for school or play.

Mom could be testy with Pop's evangelists. Once Oral Roberts mailed her a fund-raising letter addressing her as "Dear Sister Henderson" and warning that the end of his ministry was near if he didn't raise millions of dollars soon.

"I'm not his sister," Mom scoffed, and tossed the letter in the trash.

That sort of revolt was remarkable because Pop counted on Oral Roberts to heal his double hernia during his weekly TV healing service. Pop sat with his hand on the TV, as Oral had commanded, while Oral beseeched God. "Heal, heal, heal, for the love of Jesus, heal Thy people!" Oral screamed.

But Pop's hernia only enlarged and had to be controlled by increasingly elaborate trusses.

After he died, Mom confided in me that she thought Pop was "too religious."

And the line about Caspar somebody.

No matter, I concluded.

Pop to her was a husband. A husband was a husband. And that's where you left it. She cared for her husband, raised his kids, tidied his house, and was a comfort to him. She loved him in her way. Divorce was unthinkable and unspeakable.

And a son was a son.

Mom was there for this elder son, and for all her kids. At my grade school trumpet solos, at high school honor roll presentations, at football band marches where I paraded down the field as a duck-footed drum major in a fake rabbit fur hat, at track meets where I regularly finished no better than second in the quarter mile and developed a hernia trying for first—Mom was there watching.

Through high school she tutored me nightly in geometry, algebra, and trigonometry.

"What good is all this!" I hollered at her.

"It helps you think," she explained, offering her justification for a lifetime of math teaching.

"This stuff isn't about thinking! It's rules and memorizing!"

"Just do your best, Bill," she said calmly.

"Can *you* think?" I demanded.

She didn't bother to answer.

In high school I was thinking about Emerson and Thoreau. Doing my best had come to mean, to me, finding the Truth and discovering the real God that people didn't know about yet, until I completed my investigations and told them the secret.

I started the Philosophy Club with friends. We met at the home of a woman artist, the mother of a fellow student. I told the woman artist about my difficulties in discovering the Truth.

When I told Mom about that conversation, she blew up. "You hate me! You hate me hate me hate me!" she yelled, jealous of my attraction to the woman artist who had actually read Emerson and Thoreau. "You're just a little tin god!" Mom wailed. She knew that I was leaving her.

But it took me a long time to find the Truth. After her scream of rejection, Mom gave up trying to follow me on my trip.

Her calm returned. This time the calm was a wall and I was on the other side, dancing for her attention. A boy mad for a woman's love.

I had done my best. But she didn't seem convinced that I had done anything at all: divorced, the first divorce in her family, or in Pop's, going back forever; self-employed at a publishing job that was more like unemployed; a childless libertine.

Up and down the rows of boxes for Waldenbooks and B. Dalton I trudged, while she dozed.

The sun was setting, and it was time I called Bonnie about the abortion.

What difference did it make whether the kid was mine or the one-night-stand's? A kid was a kid. I should stop this abortion now. But how? Bonnie wouldn't agree to cancel it. She was an associate editor at a magazine of note. She wanted to be a senior editor, not a mom. She had places to rise to—such was our logic in the seventies.

I'd have to think more about this.

Mom and I had dinner at the Formica-covered table in the

kitchen. To her, abortion was not an option, just as murder was not an option. It was unmentionable. So I didn't bring it up.

I went to bed on the couch in the den in front of the TV, a glass in my hand.

Down the hall, Mom left her bedroom door open a crack, as she had done for thirty-six years, so she could hear if one of her children called to her in the night.

I drank my wine and watched my TV and finally slept.

I did not call Bonnie.

The next morning Bonnie had her abortion. There would be no child, no matter who the father was.

Now, dying in Bryn Mawr Hospital, Mom seemed to fall in love with the young blond nurse, Walter, who carried her to a chair, when her sheets were changed, and carried her to the toilet, before she became too weak for either chair or toilet.

"Walter, Walter!" she'd call.

She would need her IV lines straightened, or her position in bed adjusted, or a pain shot. She'd smile at Walter as he appeared in her room, a strong, clean, wholesome vision.

I tucked my notebook in my hip pocket and watched their courtship. I wondered if Walter had a family and children. Weren't all male nurses gay? Should I bring this to her attention?

Instead, I held up a four-column book review from the *Philadelphia Inquirer*. It praised the latest *Pushcart Prize* anthology that I had edited and published—and boxed in her driveway. It was a front-page book section feature with a large photo of me. I held the photo close to her and then read the review, but she seemed too weak to respond.

"You see, you brought up an OK son," I said, and moved the headline closer to her half-open eyes.

I thought it would make her feel good about her life, since her son had been well reviewed.

"Walter," she murmured.

"Walter!" I hollered, rushing into the hall to find him. He helped her roll onto her side.

What I really wanted to say to her, flat out, was, "You are the greatest mom that ever was."

But I resisted saying that. It seemed a death comment, an admission of what was happening to her. A last definition. The final letting go. I didn't want to let her go, and she didn't know how to let go.

For weeks she hung on, struggling to raise her hand to her mouth and feed herself, but never quite able; greeting her many visitors with a smile and attempts at a wave; fighting to form words; often hallucinating.

My sister Ruth mentioned that she lived, as always, for her children. If we left her alone, we might help her let go. But leaving her was impossible. Her three children were with her always, holding her hands, waiting for her to become conscious briefly, saying all the I-Love-Yous that we had neglected to say for years since puberty.

Sitting at her bedside, so close but so distant, I willed myself to enter her mind. What was it like to be dying? I wanted to be there in death with her, to think what she thought, feel what she felt.

Often I realized how easily I could end it for her. A pillow over her face for a few minutes. Nobody would know. Not even her.

Then I would worry that I might indeed kill her, not with a pillow but by helping her drink her juice. She was becoming too weak to swallow, and I had a horror of drowning her by draining the cup too quickly into her mouth.

It was difficult enough to accept that I was feeding my own mother by hand, she who had so often fed me.

"Take care of the baby," she whispered.

"What baby?" I asked, hoping she remembered the child I had promised.

"What baby?" I asked at her ear.

She tried to smile at me. It was a joke. She was the baby.

Then she sank back into what I often feared was permanent babbling.

18

"When was I born?" she asked Ruth.

"1906, Mom."

"And when did I die?"

She asked me to telephone Bob at work in Philadelphia. I held the receiver to her mouth. "I want you to know I died at 1:30 today," she told Bob, keeping him informed politely.

She lay back and asked Ruth when the services began.

"What services?" Ruth asked.

"Whatever services you and your Jewish friends want to give me."

Then she seemed to return again. "I get so confused."

"You've never been so weak before," Ruth said.

"I've never been dying before."

"The doctors don't know that for sure," I broke in quickly. "They never said that!"

"Dying is no joke," Mom said, ignoring me.

She slept.

Soon she woke up and looked at me directly. "Do you have a clean shirt?" she demanded. She had remembered that I was leaving for a day in New York and to her New York always meant a clean shirt.

When I returned from the city that evening, she was gone again into babble. She would start a sentence and get lost in it. I would try to finish the sentence for her, but she would have forgotten where she started it.

I grew bored and irritated as the weeks went on.

At another time she woke and told Walter: "I just died."

"That's not so, Mrs. Henderson." Walter said. "You know why? Because I'm no angel."

Mom chuckled. Walter adjusted the bed and lowered the slats on my side of it. She commented mysteriously: "We have to fix the crib. It is important that we fix the crib."

"What crib?" I broke in, hoping again that she referred to the promised grandchild. "Do you mean the bars on your bed or a real crib?" I tried.

Perhaps it had been another joke. She was the child, this was the crib.

"I'm so confused," she said.

"I will fix the crib, Mom, for the baby, for the new baby on that family tree."

She was the only one, including all the aunts and uncles and cousins, and in Pop's family too, who had any memory of our ancestors. After Pop died, I was desperate to make some contact with my past, and asked her to outline a family tree for Pop and herself on paper. She did.

She was the keeper of all our pasts from the Revolutionary War onward. Nobody else cared.

Reverend Waldermülder arrived in her room and announced his brand of immortality. "You are going on a long trip, Dorothy. A great adventure. It is a glorious time for you."

I was upset with Watermelon's pronouncement. It was the death sentence I had been trying to avoid. Even her doctors would admit to her only that she was holding her own.

Mom was quiet, apparently not conscious.

Then she burped.

"Excuse me," she apologized.

She drifted off briefly. Then, "Did you come for Bill's marriage?"

Instead of my marriage, he launched into the Twenty-third Psalm and left her a tape recording of the previous Sunday's service at Bryn Mawr Presbyterian Church, including his sermon.

In the hall outside her room, I demanded once again that he produce a celebration of eternal life for her funeral, and not a canned Presbyterian production. That's what would honor her. Not his pep talks about "glorious adventures," as if she were a female Captain Video.

"I am at peace with the Lord," she had said twice in that week. And she was.

"I want to go to heaven," she repeated.

Since her body wouldn't let her go to heaven yet, she imagined: "I've got to catch a plane at 7:30 tonight. The pilot needs training. The airport needs renovation."

Was she referring to her beloved minister—the pilot?

Was the church the airport that needed fixing?

More bedside parables.

In short moments of consciousness, she told us that all she wanted was for her kids to get some peace. She was sorry for the inconvenience she was causing us.

One evening after Ruth had returned briefly to Berkeley to be with her husband and children, Bob sat on one side of her bed, and I on the other. We held her hands. "My boys have such strong grips," Mom said.

In my other hand was the notebook.

Within the notebook I wondered where Mom's bravery and kindness came from in hours like this. If from God, then I would believe in God that second. But, I wrote, I had never been able to find the source.

At times, I wanted to make her a deity. She whom I so often criticized for her perpetual giving of herself to her family, her students, her church, her charities. She had given away her entire self, I had complained in a journal years earlier.

Back then I wanted a woman of funk and flash. She was too boring then for the son who now waited by her bedside and learned the meaning of awe.

Funk and flash? Of what value whatsoever?

Here was real courage.

Here was love that didn't quit.

Here was faith that never doubted.

Here was a human being who knew where immortality was.

That's why I sat next to her bed and tried to capture her last days in a notebook.

Her doctor had said an extraordinary thing, this man who had seen hundreds of people die. He was supposed to be hardened. And even he couldn't bring himself to admit what was happening. "She will never be herself again, that independent cheerful person."

Like me, he seemed unable to say the word "death."

Then he added, "I love her."

I jotted this down, adding, "These moments cannot be obliterated by time."

I wrote my notes furtively with a Bic pen, my notebook in my lap, when I thought she was sleeping. I didn't want her to imagine I was writing her obituary.

In scribbling these notes, I participated in her strength, even as a biographer draws some glory from a subject. She wouldn't understand that. This paper honor, this notebook immortality, this private proclamation of mine, she wouldn't understand, I thought.

Mom's perpetual notebooks were kept by God.

Mom honored people by deeds, not notes. She didn't preach or spin morality tales. Her lived life was her message. Her theory of a human being was the person in front of her.

So I kept my notebook below the level of the bed.

I wrote:

They overradiated the incision from her breast operation 12 years ago. It never healed. Open to the breastbone now. The chemo killed her hair and her eyelids are gone, eyes never closed, half-open always. It's too hot for the wig. It's by her bedside. The chemo ruined her immune system. Pneumonia now. Lungs filling with fluid. Drowning. An oxygen tube in her nose, catheter running urine into 'her purse,' as she calls it. IV bottle drips morphine, dextrose, antibiotics into her arm. Even as she dies, the old IV needle holes in her arm heal and the scabs drop off. She is outliving the gift plants on her nightstand. She won't let go.

On her last day, her doctor ordered that antibiotics be stopped. They weren't helping the pneumonia and only raised her temperature, he said.

He ordered the aspiration to remove fluid from her lungs.

The pain was worse. "Nurse, nurse, nurse," she called, barely able to move her lips. It was only the second time in twelve years that I had heard her complain of the pain. The other time was when she had said "shit."

As Walter moved her to her side in the constant battle against bedsores, her hospital gown fell open and I saw my mother naked for the first time. Her flesh hung limp from a body that was still as handsome as it seemed in her senior yearbook photo from the 1924 West Philadelphia High School for Girls. She was a tall, dark-haired, dark-eyed hockey player in a short skirt, with a hint of a smile. The caption announced her favorite adage was "Oh gee!" and her motto "Weary hearts by Thee are lightened, struggling souls by Thee are strengthened, clouds of fear asunder rifted."

She was named "Best Mathematician."

Under the yearbook in Mom's drawer was a small bundle of Pop's letters to her, and hers to him—fragments of a long friendship and a long courtship.

They had lived a few miles from each other since birth. They were church friends in the 1920s and became more than friends in September 1931 when she thanked him for a ride from Philadelphia to Westfield, New Jersey, where she taught high school. "I will be back in the city next weekend. If you are in the city, too, you might call me maybe—yes?"

After that, silence.

There were Christmas cards from her in 1934 and 1936 signed only "Dorothy Galloway."

In January 1937, she signed a note "Dot."

In May 1937 she wrote:

I want to smile and sing and tell everybody how wonderful everything is. On the other hand this new feeling that I'm experiencing is so young and tender and precious that I want to keep it close within my heart so that it can be nurtured with reverent prayer and wise meditation.

Never have I felt such a great need for Christ in my life and never has His presence and His love been so real and powerful for me. Whatever else you've done for me, dear, you've brought me closer to Him.

In a letter from October 1937: "It's been a rather cold and damp day, but I've been so happy—singing and humming all the while and just beaming all over. 'Cause why? You know, darlin'—the most wonderful man in the world has asked me to marry him ..."

Reading these letters, I waited for her to mention the prospect of children, a family, the dream of her firstborn. But she never did. Perhaps that would have scared him off, like saying "sex" out loud.

He had bolted once, worried about Luke 20, verses 35 and 36: "But they which shall be accounted worthy to obtain that world and the resurrection from the dead, neither marry nor are given in marriage."

She coaxed him back with Matthew 19, verses 4 to 6: "Have you not read that He which made them at the beginning made them male and female ... and for this cause shall a man leave father and mother and shall cleave to his wife and they shall be one flesh."

"Flesh" was as close to "sex" as she dared.

God was the joy of their impending marriage.

Just before their wedding, she wrote: "God's power is so great. I feel like a little child reaching up for His helping hand—and oh, the joy and feeling of relief and the feeling of power to do all things through Him that come down to me. He will help us solve our problems. On our wedding day, as always, He will be with us and where our strength fails, His will hold us steadfast."

After the morphine was added to her IV bottle, the nurse listened to her chest. I was asked to step into the hall while the nurse hooked up the mouthpiece and aspirated her lungs. When I returned, Mom was sitting up, gasping for air, in agony, her eyes staring in two directions.

It was then that I grabbed the doctor and said, "I want her *out*." I repeated it, not daring to define the meaning of "out."

I wondered if I would start screaming and never stop screaming.

The doctor gave his morphine instructions to a nurse and left.

The extra morphine began to drip into her arm about two P.M.

"You're a great mom, the greatest there was," I finally managed to tell her, appalled that I used the word *was* and not *is*.

Her eyes were shut in the lidless way. She breathed in short bursts. "Ahhhh," she answered me.

Cry of pain, death rattle, acknowledgment that she had heard my summation of her life? I'd never know.

"Are you in pain?" I asked.

A nurse nearby said, "Semicomatose."

I persuaded Bob to go home and rest. He would return and stay with her through the night.

Bob kissed her cheek and bent his cheek to her mouth as he did every night. That way she could feel that she had kissed Bob back, although she was unable to move her lips.

Bob left for a few hours.

Through the window blinds, the September sun headed for the horizon. I held her hand and watched the sun as she gasped and slept.

Suddenly she shouted, "Let's go!"

She grabbed her covers and yanked them off.

"Let's go *now*!" she demanded.

"Where to?" I asked, amazed, as if I were witnessing her resurrection.

"To the beauty parlor!" she said.

I was astounded. And helpless.

"We will do that soon," I promised, replacing her covers.

I found her wig comb in the nightstand drawer and a can of talcum powder. I dusted her bald scalp with the talcum and began to comb the few hairs left, trying to calm her.

Maybe she could dream that she was at the beauty parlor and I was the beautician. I combed and combed.

She shut her eyes and seemed to enjoy it.

Again, she drifted off.

I took her hand.

She whispered something. I put my ear next to her mouth. "Let's go."

"Go where, Mom?"

"Home."

"You want to go home?"

"Yes."

"Are you sure?" I looked into her eyes. She was alert. Determined.

"Positive!"

She grabbed my hair with her hand. "I want to go home with *you!*"

On the phone, the doctor said it was indeed possible to take her home, but "she will die sooner." He finally said the word *die.* There seemed to be a problem with bringing her IV bottle home with us. The doctor and I agreed to make arrangements in the morning for the short trip.

I raised the back of her bed and opened the shades so she could see the sun.

I planned a backyard party for Mom, with wine and music and dancing, a wake before she died. All her kids and all her friends would be there.

She asked for a drink, so I held a cup of juice to her lips. I waited. But she could not move her lips to swallow. I put the cup back down.

She seemed to doze again.

"Such incredible rebound power . . . she goes down and comes back. But each time she goes down further . . ." I scribbled below the level of the mattress.

"What's that?" She was awake again. "What are you writing down there?"

She had turned her head and was inches away from my eyes, glaring at me.

"Nothing, Mom. It's nothing."

"Give me that!" she snapped.

She grabbed for the notebook and I moved it away.

These were her last words to me.

I thought about handing her the notebook. She couldn't read it anyway without her glasses. But I offered instead, "Mom, I'm writing down what you say here. I want the world to know what a great person you are."

She turned her head away. She lay back.

She sighed.

Again, she slept.

I called Bob and told him about our coming-home plans, and the living wake.

After the sun set, two young women nurses appeared in her door and said they needed to change the dressing on the festering breast incision.

Mom lifted up both of her arms and smiled a greeting to them. "Hello, how are you?" she exclaimed, and took their hands in hers.

"Feeling better, Mrs. Henderson?" they asked.

"Much better."

She adored them as if they were her own sweet cheerleaders.

I left the room, as instructed by the nurses, and went to meet Bob downstairs.

When he and I returned to the room, Mom had slipped under again.

"Do you still want to go home tomorrow?" I asked her.

She raised an arm, extended her fingers to me, attempted to speak and let her arm drop soundlessly.

She slept.

I said good night to her still face and left. Halfway down the hall, I remembered that I had forgotten to kiss her.

I decided not to go back. She would be sleeping anyway. I would see her tomorrow for the trip home.

An hour later Bob called. "I think Mom is dying now."

Through the night I sped back to her then spoke my final feeble words to her corpse, hoping that maybe, as the nurse had said, hearing is the last sense to go.

"Mom, it's me. I'm here, Mom. I'm here now, Mom!"

I kissed her good night.

Too late my words. Too late my kiss.

Her final comment to me: a sigh.

II

New York, 1978

2

Plato's

TO BE ADMITTED into Plato's Retreat, a public orgy celebrated in the late seventies, I needed a date. Unlike other popular orgies, this was a high-class deal, for couples only.

Plato's had been featured in the *Village Voice*, editorialized against in *Time*, and photographed in loving masturbatory detail in *Playboy*. Sex was entertainment (conception a bore), and Plato's was the epitome of what was coming to be called a "lifestyle." It was also the chat of all the literary cocktail parties I attended, a place to say you had been. And tonight I was going.

It was a casual decision made over a drink at a new members' gathering of PEN, the writers' club. Susan, also a new member, and an occasional sex pal, asked if I'd tried Plato's. I hadn't. We took a cab to the Ansonia Hotel on Broadway and walked down a dark side street where single men needing a date muttered to passing women, "Going to Plato's?" A gauntlet of mutters.

Under a striped awning, Susan and I descended cement steps as if into somebody's cellar. A cashier in a cage invited us to read the rules of membership she handed us. Then she told us to sign a pledge that we were at least twenty-one and not prostituting ourselves or selling drugs.

After we paid our membership fee of twenty-five dollars each plus a five-dollar admission fee, we were allowed into the underground cavern and its swimming pool, dance room, private party chambers, and hall of a hundred mattresses. The walls were frescoed with broken columns and figures in Roman togas gulping grapes and wine, as if this business were justified by historical precedent.

A hostess wearing a towel directed us past a smorgasbord table of steaming food and bowls of punch to the locker room. There another toweled hostess handed us each a locker key with a bit of elastic on it to tie to our ankles. From now on, it was expected that we would have no clothes pockets for the keys, although a sign in the locker room announced "dress optional," and several couples toured the cavern in street clothes.

Susan and I stripped and wrapped ourselves in the single towel provided to each of us—mine around my waist, Susan's around her breasts. Keys on ankles, we moved out into the cellar, past a naked girl passing a joint with two guys in muted conversation.

At the swimming pool, a dozen naked people sat by the side while one or two swam and a girl sucked the cock of an older man standing in the shallow end.

Except for the splashing of the swimmers and the sound of distant dance music, the pool was quiet.

The mattress hall too was silent. No whoops or hollers here. People were either splayed out with one or more partners or resting up individually for the next encounter.

In one corner of the hall, a fellow was being worked on by a girl who seemed anxious that he might never be ready again. She sucked with fury. He dangled. I felt sorry for him. To be unable to get it up in public must have been a serious humiliation.

Susan and I sat on a mattress with our backs against a floor-to-ceiling mirror and observed the hall.

I had always thought of fucking as a violent exercise. But this hall, filled with scores of mattresses and a crowd of fornicators, was curiously still. All the motions, seen from across the room, were minor ins and outs and ups and downs. In the dim light they were hardly noticeable. Now and then somebody would climb up or flop off. That was major action.

Susan lifted my towel.

Embarrassed, I asked her what she was doing. Being naked in public was a worst nightmare.

"Everybody else is doing it," she smiled and got started.

After several drinks at the pub earlier, I wasn't all that prompt to spring up. I worried that I too might be floppy in public. Then I worried that I might come too soon, and have no more business here. To stall, I reached out to the breast of an obese woman next to me. While Susan shuddered and played with me, I concentrated on the gross lady.

A guy in a towel crawled across several mattresses and with a motion of his head, asked Susan if he had her permission. She nodded and left my cock. With a deft movement, he quickly entered her. She held my hand while he worked on her.

During this break, I asked the fat lady beside me and her equally round partner if they had any grass in their locker. "We did that *before* we came," she snapped, as if I ought to know the etiquette, whether I was new here or not.

Abruptly the guy was finished with Susan. He pulled out without apparent orgasm or any sound—merely a nod to her and to me. He refastened his towel and crawled back across the mattresses into the twilight.

I spotted a girl I liked the looks of in a group nearby and I asked her if she'd like to.

"OK," she said.

While we fucked, she quizzed me. "You'd never believe how old I am."

"How old?" I smiled down at her.

"I'm not telling." She giggled.

After a while, I thanked her and moved on to her girlfriend next to her, who had just concluded a bout with two guys. I no-

ticed a couple next to us, a black man and a white woman en-
twined in the sixty-nine position. Her vulva was swollen and
enormous. They were motionless. I thought they might be out
cold.

Susan scampered over to sit by me. I thanked the girl of guess-
my-age and withdrew and sat with Susan against the mirror
again.

The girl I had just left sat on a fellow's cock and rode him up
and down. "Eiiiiiiiiiyi!" she began. Louder and louder she
screamed.

The patrons stopped what they were doing and looked at her
in amazement. Some shook their heads, as if disapproving. She
had lost her cool.

Susan and I left the mattress for a tour.

Back at the swimming pool we watched a couple attempting
to screw in the deep water without success, and we chatted with
a young lifeguard. He said that for the first few days his job was
interesting, but now it was just a job. Nothing ever happened
here. He was sick of sex. He couldn't wait to get home.

Looking out across the silent basement—the girl had finally
stopped screaming—I said I knew what he meant. The triumph
of the sexual revolution? There had to be more here than this.

Wrapped in our towels, Susan and I headed for the private
party closets.

We passed an argument in progress at the door to the mattress
hall. The middle-aged matron, dressed in a dark blue suit and
guarding the door, was forbidding entrance to a tall thin girl
dressed only in knee-length boots. "Sorry, dear, not in here.
Against insurance regulations."

The girl protested, but the matron was firm.

"Why the no boots rule?" I wondered to Susan.

"Maybe they're afraid she'll step on somebody," Susan
pointed out.

Susan and I had to wait for a private closet. They seemed to be
filled.

While waiting in the passage outside the closets, I read a

posted complaint: "Why do they want to shut us down? Who are we hurting? Write to your congressman. Tell him we are having a good time. That's all. —The Management, Plato's Retreat."

"I hear it's Mafia-backed," said Susan.

The private party closets were so dark we couldn't tell by opening the door a crack if they were occupied. Impatiently I did push one door open, and a girl shouted: "Watch the ankle! I hurt it skiing!"

But, politely, she and her partner shoved over to share their chamber. After a few minutes, my eyes adjusted and I could see that it was the sixty-nine couple.

I asked him, after working with Susan a bit on our side of the closet, if he'd like to switch.

"Sure," he agreed.

We hopped around each other and he climbed on top of Susan, and I mounted his friend.

While Susan moaned beside me, I asked the girl under me where she was from.

"The University of Massachusetts."

"What do you study there?"

"English Lit...You?"

"A publisher."

Later, we tried to form a foursome, but it got too complicated and we went back to our original one-on-one.

An hour later, Susan, who was two orgasms ahead of me for the evening, whispered, "I've had it. I want to go home. Let me finish you."

I suggested one more turn in the mattress hall. I wasn't about to come to my first orgy and come inside the girl I came with.

We left our sixty-nine friends without good-bye and returned to the hall. "He wasn't very good," Susan confided. "An Oreo cookie, white at heart." I wondered what that comment meant about the abilities of white guys in Susan's estimation.

Back in the mattress hall gloom, I looked for a previous partner, the one who asked me how old she was. Maybe I could guess her age. Over forty, probably.

Susan engaged herself with a paunchy bald fellow in the middle of the hall while his date sucked her breast at his orders, and another guy waddled up and proffered his semi-erect cock for a lick. Susan briefly obliged him but three bodies were more than she could efficiently handle. She returned her affections to the paunchy guy.

In a corner, currently sucking a cock, I discovered the girl of uncertain age. Since this was my second time—indeed I'd had a conversation with her—I didn't feel that I had to observe orgy manners. I hiked up behind her and engaged.

She stopped sucking, peered around to see who it was this time, smiled at me, and returned to her present cock. When I came, she looked over her shoulder again and winked at me. I had complimented her by donating my sperm in her. Guys only had so many ejaculations per orgy.

I wandered around searching for Susan. Near the smorgasbord I spotted a blonde in bra and panties, her hair shining in a spotlight. She was laughing happily and talking with two women. I liked her hair. I loved her laugh. She seemed to be the only out-loud, happy person here.

But there was no time to talk. I was exhausted. The mystery laughing blonde would have to wait.

Susan and I found each other and left.

While we waited for a cab upstairs, we heard the sounds below piped in for the Ansonia's doorman's pleasure. Now and then there was a moan or a yelp.

Susan said, "I hope we don't get any diseases."

"What diseases?" I asked. "They've discovered them all. They can cure anything with penicillin."

To me, Plato's had been like a surreal primitive church.

We were all naked in God's sight, and in each other's.

The hugs and the fucks were there for all. Nobody cared what your job or your position was; or your color or age or your name. Fat or skinny, tall or short or in between. Plato's was for everybody equally. Nobody was rejected, or jilted, or jealous.

Later, I warned myself in my journal, "A hump is not a hug. Fucking is not loving. Nobody else there thought about God except you."

I recalled that distant Sunday school where we children sang, "Jesus loves the little children. All the children of the world. Red and yellow, black and white, they are precious in His sight."

And we children were all loved and loved others equally.

Such simple and innocent ideas.

My relics from God's house.

3

Ruth

BONNIE TELEPHONED on February 22, 1978. She seemed to have forgotten her abortion of our probable child a few months before. She said she needed an escort for a fancy literary party. I could be that escort, she said, but only if I promised to get lost as soon as we arrived so she could hitch up with somebody else.

She explained it was a black-tie event. Since I didn't own a tux, I could probably get away with my turtleneck and blue blazer, she said.

I waited for Bonnie in the sports bar under the Time-Life building. It was decorated with giant photographs of sports celebrities, another basement, like Plato's, pretending that it wasn't a basement at all.

At the bar, I polished my old black loafers with spit and a paper napkin, expecting something grand from this evening. I didn't know what. I had been drinking for several nights straight and was feeling it. The *New York Times* had discovered my little publishing company dedicated to independence from corporate publishing, and I had discovered the literary cocktail party. At these parties I tweaked the establishment by flogging Pushcart's *Publish-It-Yourself Handbook*, a complete guide to doing without that very establishment. It had sold over 50,000 copies in many printings.

This party, Bonnie had said, was for James Jones's post-humously published novel, *Whistle*. I had read only one novella by Jones, something about a pistol. I hadn't read *Whistle* or any of his earlier books, but once I had sat next to him and his wife, Gloria, at a Bridgehampton pub. They talked about private school for their daughter Kaylie. Nice people. I had listened and said nothing to him. A year later, he was dead.

Bonnie arrived and we walked to Park Avenue.

Jones's publisher had hired the entire Armory at Park and Sixty-ninth Street. The hall, used for drill practice and the storage of weapons and army trucks, was partitioned off into a dining room and several bars.

Bonnie ditched me soon, as promised, and I stood alone at the first bar nearest the door, working on my hangover with white wine.

When Norman Mailer strolled up to the bar, I was into my third wine. "Have you ever heard of me?" I demanded. A joke.

He hadn't. But he hung around at the bar to talk with other people he had heard of.

I stopped counting my drinks.

The elevator door opened and flashbulbs flared. Lauren Bacall had arrived and her press agent, perhaps judging that welcoming trumpets would have been too garish and obvious, had made sure she was announced with dozens of flashbulbs.

Behind her was a blond woman who looked like Ellen Burstyn, the actress. I'd seen this woman some place before, but couldn't remember where. In the movies, probably, if she was indeed Ellen Burstyn.

The woman waited until the flashbulbs let up for Lauren Bacall and then moved from the elevator and down the receiving line of Gloria Jones and the Jones children.

I moved back to Norman Mailer, continuing my joke. "You know, you really *should* know me. Here's my card." This time he laughed.

Woody Allen was at my elbow. I congratulated him on our mutual good taste in unpretentious dress. In a room of black ties, we wore the only two turtlenecks.

"At least there are two honest guys here," I said. Another joke.

Somebody tapped me on the shoulder. "There's a lady here who wants to meet you," he said.

I didn't recognize the guy, but the lady was the Ellen Burstyn look-alike. "She was standing over there by herself," the introducer said, and mentioned her name. Her hair was bright blond and, like those of the other women here, her dress was not standard issue. A statement of some sort.

Her smile, though, was open and uncalculating. A rare smile for New York. I had seen that smile somewhere before.

Her name was not Ellen Burstyn. But I quickly forgot what it was.

"Maybe we should see each other after this is over," I said, and handed her my business card. I told her she had never heard of me and that I was there as an uninvited date. Undercover.

"Me, too," she smiled and added something about doing a TV co-host and "To Tell The Truth." Bumping into Cleveland Amory on the street that afternoon. I couldn't hear her. I was surrounded by babbling mouths. Her mouth alone wanted to be kissed.

"Didn't I see you at Plato's . . . ?" I started, recalling the blonde at the buffet.

But there was no time to go into all that.

Twenty feet away was Walter Cronkite, and I had something very important to tell him.

He and I had met at a great moment in human history, the moon landing. In 1969 I was married to an ex-nun who had abandoned Jesus for Wittgenstein and would soon abandon me for an ex-convict. We were living in a graduate-student barracks in Princeton while she studied her new mentor, Wittgenstein. I was trying to start writing a commercial thriller about a sniper who shot up a baby parade in Ocean City, New Jersey. I called it *Sniper*.

Walter Cronkite commented for CBS.

In our barracks, I watched TV.

Together we saw Neil Armstrong step down from the moon-lander and say, "That's one small step for (a) man, a giant leap for mankind."

I plowed through the room, spilling my white wine and hugged Walter Cronkite gently. "I want you to know, Walter, that when you cried about the moon landing, I cried too. I loved you for your tears. You are no fake!"

There. I'd said it.

I spun off into the dark hall.

The place was jammed with gods. Gods of this, gods of that.

Wilfrid Sheed and John Updike sat at a table talking. I flopped down at one end of the table, waved at Wilfrid, whom I had met once, and wondered about all of this.

"These are my people," I concluded to myself. "I belong here. We have all come through. We stuck to it. We did not subside into mediocrity."

Then I recalled that I was just a date, meant to get lost.

No matter.

Bonnie arrived. It was time for dinner.

So far, she said, the party had been a bust for her. She would persevere in her hunt for a bedmate, but for now we should sit down if I was sober enough to handle dinner.

I remember a big dim room, with dozens of round tables, and a small rostrum with a reading light at the head table. There was food of some sort, and there were speeches, and Jones's editor, Burroughs Mitchell, asked for tributes to Jim from the floor. William Styron spoke and then Ralph Ellison, who would not stop talking.

I tiptoed to the bar just outside the room and stood alone waiting for Ellison to finish.

Then "Ellen Burstyn" was again beside me.

I kissed her cheek.

She kissed me softly on the lips.

Too drunk to imagine any other way to put it, I asked, "Wanna fuck?"

She shook her head, smiled, and kissed me again.

"Like to go home with me?" I tried again.

Somebody hushed us. I was talking too loudly. Ellison had sat down and I had become the floor show. A spectacle.

I exited to the men's room.

When I wandered back, the blond woman had disappeared.

I set off in search of her. But the building was vast—a block long on each side.

Far from the ongoing speeches, a woman I'd seen on TV was talking with somebody on a couch near some armored personnel carriers.

I was about to go when the woman was suddenly left alone on the couch. It was Ruth Carter Stapleton, evangelist and healer from Plains, Georgia. And sister of the president of the United States.

Why was she sitting by herself now ignored? Didn't this snooty crowd approve of President Carter? He who had kissed Brezhnev? A Christian kiss for a monster? That would have been a big hoo-haa with this bunch.

And they probably didn't approve of Ruth, either. She had written a book about her beer-swilling, gas-pumping brother, Billy. Too unliterary for this lot?

Not for me.

As with Walter, I had essential information to convey to Ruth.

I placed my glass on the coffee table in front of her and sat down hard. "Hi! I'm Bill Henderson."

"Ruth Stapleton," she said.

"I know. I know who you are. You're the only evangelist I've ever seen for real in person since Billy Graham. Ocean City, New Jersey, about 1948. He was in a big tent by the boardwalk and you could hear the ocean breaking outside the tent. My dad took me there. He was very religious, believed in faith healing. This was a really big moment. Billy Graham was new in town. New everywhere, for that matter. And my dad and I sat on wooden folding chairs in the back of the circus tent and my dad let me sit on the aisle side so I could see straight up the aisle to the microphone where Billy spoke."

I stopped for a breath in my rambles.

"Yes?" she smiled, encouraging me.

"You want to hear more?"

I stared into her eyes, unsure.

"Certainly."

"My dad was one of the few guys I ever met anywhere who really believed. I mean really really believed. No doubts. He talked to Jesus all the time. Even on the job. The world around him hardly even existed."

A crowd was pushing out of the dining area. Some of the diners came our way.

I found I was holding Ruth's hand.

I didn't care what the others thought.

She tightened her grip on my hand, so that I wouldn't pull away. "Tell me more about you and your dad."

"It seemed like we were the good guys, my dad and I and Billy Graham and everybody in the tent. I'd heard of the Communists and I was only seven years old so I didn't know what all that was, except it was evil. And we were good, and if I looked up I might see Jesus and His angels riding like cowboys across the clouds. Our guys!" I hooted.

I held her hand tighter.

"All those summers in Ocean City my mom and dad took us to church twice on Sunday, morning and evening, and outside the windows of the chapel I'd see the sinners dragging their rafts to and from the beach when they should have been in church with us. We would have to fix that. I sang with my dad and mom so those sinners could hear us and be saved. All summer long we sang."

I gazed into Ruth's eyes. Again I began to sing: "Trust and obey, for there's no other way. . ."

She knew the words. She joined me.

In the middle of that humming, laughing, drinking, clever mob, we squeezed each other's hands and we sang: "Trust and obey, for there's no other way, to be happy in Jesus, but to trust and obey."

When we finished the last verse in our solitude, I was tearing up. I had no more words left. I bent over and kissed her on the lips.

And she kissed me back.

Then I knew I was terribly, dangerously drunk and had to get out of there without crashing headfirst onto the table in front of us.

" 'Bye," I managed, and lurched up, holding onto the couch arm and her hand. She steadied me.

I realized that I must not open my mouth again. I had said all that I was permitted to say at this party.

I loped through the celebrities, hoping to spot my Ellen Burstyn. But she was nowhere.

So I left, stumbling down the Armory's stone stairs onto Park Avenue.

In that cold February night, three words began to rearrange themselves in my brain. "If Ruth's God is Love; then Love is God."

That's simple. Who could deny that Love is God?

Sure you could deny it in reverse. You could say to Ruth there is no God. Therefore God is not Love.

Or there are horrors in the universe. Therefore, God is not Love. But love? Love does not make earthquakes, bombs, holocausts. Love is God. That works.

Wordplay. I played with the words.

"Find me one person who would deny that love is everything for everybody," I said, looking up and down the empty sidewalk.

And what is sin?

Sin is the withholding of love from another person. From yourself, too. That's what sin is.

And since we all do this to each other all the time— withhold love—we are all sinners.

"Sin is failing to love!" I shouted, startled at this revelation.

On that early morning street, thirty years after Pop took me to see Billy Graham in his tent, I finally understood something about God, Love, and Sin. About Jesus.

Then I was simply amazed.

"I just kissed the sister of the president of the United States on the lips!" I whispered to myself.

"And she kissed me back!"

4

Annie

"MILLS HOTEL FOR MEN, Number 2" was engraved in stone over the entrance to the Bleecker Street building where I lived. Theodore Dreiser once lived there too, but, until a recent remodeling, the Mills Hotel had been a flophouse. A few years earlier a resident wino had pitched a table out a high window and killed a pedestrian. It made the papers.

My sixth-floor studio apartment faced west. Between buildings I could glimpse the smokestacks of ships on the Hudson River, but not the river itself. In an unshaded window across the street two naked guys often touch-fucked under a light bulb, adoring each other's bodies and inviting neighbors to adore them. In the apartment under me a woman wailed orgasmically every morning, but I never heard another voice in her room. Tourists crowded the streets below, seeking a whiff of fifties bohemia, but only a few coffeehouses with faded photos of Beat greats remained from those days.

I was a publisher with four titles on my list—the self-published novel I had consumed   years in writing; the handbook that told other writers how to publish their own work, and the first two editions of my annual *Pushcart Prize* anthology of poetry, essays, and stories from little magazines and small presses.

Pushcart Press, I had named myself. The press occupied the space under the double bed. The bed filled most of the apartment and was supported by boxes of books. In good weeks, the bed sank closer to the floor as orders left, carried on my back in number one mailbags to the nearby Prince Street post office. In bad weeks, when unsold books were returned, the bed rose again, sometimes at an awkward angle.

I was poor, but honorable in my poverty. Once, at lunch with Harvey Shapiro, editor of the *New York Times Book Review*, I complained that I wouldn't mind publishing at least one bestseller.

"You couldn't," he snapped, disappointed that I had even thought of lowering myself to a bestseller.

I ran my business with an old manual typewriter and a PhoneMate answering machine that was losing its voice. I had no money for better machines and most months paying the rent was a scramble.

The PhoneMate whispered to me in falsetto one afternoon: "This is Annie McCoy. I met you at the *Whistle* party in the Armory. Do you remember? 'The real McCoy?' Blond? Call me at 348–69 . . ." and the message was cut off when the caller hung up.

A friend's voice, Jim, barely disguised. A strange joke, I thought. When I called him back, he assured me there was such a lady as Annie McCoy. I had talked to her at the *Whistle* party. "You were probably too drunk to remember," he said. For three weeks this Annie person had been searching the city for somebody who knew me. A friend of hers knew a friend of his. Jim gave me Annie's real number. I wrote it down, but after we hung up, I crumpled the paper and threw it under the bed. Nobody had a name like Annie McCoy. The real McCoy . . . I wasn't going to fall for this.

The crumpled paper ball lay under the bed with the books and was forgotten.

Weeks later I called another lady to confirm a date. And called and called, and realized I had been dismissed, discarded, dishonored. Shot down. Stood up.

I remembered the paper ball. Driven by hurt, I crawled under the bed and found it in the dust.

I called the number.

A voice answered. The voice said she was Annie McCoy.

I told the voice I would meet her at the Lion's Head on Christopher Street and I wouldn't recognize her. She said that was OK. She would remember me.

I sat at the bar and waited to be identified. For a while I was alone, and then I talked with John, a friend, while looking at the clock and wondering if I would be stood up again and if there really was an Annie McCoy after all, or if the joke had become even more elaborate.

I trusted no woman and resolved never to trust again. Dating was for laughs. I had developed a tight New York smile.

Finally a woman walked in. Ellen Burstyn. I looked at my drink, still unsure, until she walked directly to me and said, "Hi, Bill, I'm Annie."

"I wish somebody beautiful would walk in off the street and say that to me," said John, moving down the bar.

"Is your name really Annie McCoy?" I asked, with my tight smile.

She nodded. "I'm glad I finally found you."

We ordered some wine.

"Do you remember me?" Annie asked, smiling with flawless uptown teeth. From the party I recalled something about her blond-streaked hair and her fine clothes—now she wore a fluffy white sweater. I remembered when I kissed her at the party that she seemed Upper-East-Side.

I didn't like her. A rich fluff in a fluffy sweater. I wondered how long I would have to sit here.

Annie gazed constantly at me, smiling and laughing at whatever I said.

I quickly downed my wine and ordered another.

"You don't know how hard it was to find you again, Bill. I've been looking all over the whole city. Tell me about yourself."

A desperate ploy, I thought. I offered a few words to keep the conversation going until I could scram.

"I wrote a novel. Spent seven years writing it. Published it myself when nobody else would. Lost ten thousand dollars. Had a wife once, too." Maybe if I sounded like bad news, Annie would leave quicker.

"Where is the wife now?"

"I really don't know. She shacked up with an ex-con."

"An ex-con?"

"Right. It's hilarious."

"Why?"

"She's an ex-nun."

I thought this might be too much for Upper-East-Side Annie, a guy married once to an ex-nun. But she didn't blink, and kept her eyes on me. So I continued.

"She's been living with this ex-con on the Lower East Side. I was on Astor Place a few weeks ago, and I think I saw her standing on a corner near some hookers. I was in a cab, and we had stopped at a light, and I think it was her. I went back the next night and hung around with the hookers but I never saw her again."

"You were worried about her—could you call her?"

"I don't know her number. I heard she was living on East Fourth Street. I went there one night and asked a guy, a lookout I guess, if he knew her. He said he never heard of her, and the cabbie acted as if we had driven into a war zone. A drug alley, the cabbie said. He wanted out of there fast. So I quit looking."

I could have told Annie more about the ex-nun. How she found me drunk at a Philadelphia pub, a rejected first novelist of twenty-five, about to be drafted for Vietnam. About how she had just left the convent she had joined from a small town in Iowa— the only way out of that small town. About how we saved each other for seven years until it fell apart. But that was too strange for Annie, I decided.

"Did you have any kids?" Annie asked.

"No, thank God. We were lucky in that."

I ordered my fourth glass of wine and one for Annie. Maybe I could figure out an excuse to split—fake a drunk, that always worked—or maybe John would come back down the bar and I could hand Annie over to him.

"And what about your novel?" she smiled. "You published it yourself?"

"It's under my bed now. My uncle and I did it. We started a publishing company. It flopped years ago. Did my novel and a set of Horatio Alger books. You ever heard of Horatio Alger?"

I doubted it.

"Sure. He wrote boys' books. I read him, and I read Nancy Drew, too, when I was a girl. I loved Nancy Drew. I used to pretend I was Nancy Drew. A friend of mine, Pam, and I acted out Nancy's cases. There's a new book out about Nancy Drew and Horatio Alger, too."

"*Rascals at Large* by Arthur Prager," I said.

"That's it."

I was impressed. "You read *Rascals at Large?*"

"Sure," Annie said. "I loved it."

"Hard work, honesty—Alger ideas. Rebel ideas these days . . ." I was starting to ramble into my wine glass.

I was also beginning to pay attention to Annie.

No woman had ever hunted me down in a city of eight million people, and no Horatio Alger fan could be all bad.

"I just started a literary anthology," I mentioned. Published that myself, too, and suddenly I'm an authority. The *Times* called it 'a distinguished literary event.' But I'm no authority on anything. In fact, I was fired from every job I ever had—Doubleday, Putnam. Some authority. My head spins, my knees wobble from all this notice."

"What?" She looked at me without her smile and cocked her head.

Where had this confession come from? I wanted Annie to like me. Now I was the worrisome part of this date.

"Why are your knees weak from notice?" she asked, as if I had a knee disease.

I let it drop. "How about you?" I asked. "Marriage, kids, boyfriend?"

"I had a boyfriend until just before I met you at the party. He left me. We were living in Washington Heights."

"I'm sorry."

"It's OK, really. I've never been so thrilled. I'm free now! I don't have to report to anybody. My whole life has started over. I'm doing stuff I never did before!"

Where had I seen her before?

I thought again about the blonde at Plato's Retreat. Had that been Annie? But I didn't want to ask and upset her.

"A subletter. I love to keep moving, place to place," she said.

We were quiet for a while, thinking of her wonderful new freedom. Then: "You know, Bill, I'm having a midlife breakdown."

I didn't know what to say about her breakdown. She wasn't a fluff. Maybe she was crazy.

We moved to the back room. Over hamburgers and another bottle of wine, Annie sketched her life: daughter of a Mississippi doctor, finishing school, theatrical degree from Northwestern University, early acting rejections in New York, then a side business with a friend—Supergirls, an outfit that would provide any service that was legal—and a Supergirl stint on the Johnny Carson show. At age twenty-four she'd chatted with Johnny for ten minutes coast-to-coast.

But Supergirls was over. Now she was writing a book on contract, about the banana business. And she hated bananas.

I understood a little more about the breakdown, but the idea of ten minutes on the "Tonight Show" numbed me. What was that?

I told Annie my plans: I would write a memoir about my Pop and growing up in a house where we really believed in Jesus, really. Not like the usual equivocating, halfhearted suburban family. "I can't let that kind of faith just slip away and be forgotten. I have to set it on paper, Annie. I'll call my book *Love Letter to the World*, and I'm going to start writing it next week," I proclaimed.

I had just decided on the *Love Letter* title at that moment—my Pop seemed suddenly wonderful to me, a steady, kind vision in a universe of horrors.

Annie and I moved on to 55, a dive next door. Nancy Drew came up again, and *Rascals at Large*. We found Arthur Prager's number in the phone book and called him. We had just formed the Arthur Prager Fan Club, we announced when he answered, and he should come to 55 and join us. He declined. *Rascals at Large* had sold only three thousand copies and was now remaindered, he said, but he appreciated the fan club.

We were awash in booze, hamburgers, and autobiography. Again I invited Annie to my bed.

"I promised a friend I wouldn't do that with you on the first date." Annie smiled. "She said you go through women like water."

"I do?" I asked, flattered that I had a rake's reputation. I, who had been left by one ex-nun wife—swapped for a criminal—and often rejected since.

"We'll just watch TV. I'll show you my publishing office," I offered.

Holding hands, we headed out into the cold Village night.

In the office, I showed her the warehouse under the bed, where I had retrieved the paper ball only hours before. But because of the wine, I could do little on top of the bed.

Annie said it was OK. We'd just sleep. The morning would make it better.

By dawn, the wine's effects had left me. I remember a bright sunrise and her golden hair, formerly the dyed hair of a fluff, now the glory of a caring lady who had traveled downtown to my hovel in the Mills Hotel for Men, Number 2.

I made her instant coffee and an English muffin with margarine and asked her to stay for a while.

"Usually men can't wait to get rid of me afterward," Annie laughed. She seemed almost grateful.

Who would want to get rid of a girl as pretty and funny as Annie, I wondered. I worried about her nomad ways in a dangerous city.

That day we searched for a permanent place for Annie. Some new apartments were being constructed near Bleecker Street. We explored the empty rooms together.

5

Sophie

ON A SUNDAY night in November 1980, Annie and I went to a quietly boring movie in midtown. Afterward, quietly bored, I said good-bye to Annie, who was preserving her independence that night by sleeping uptown in her own bed by herself.

I walked south toward the Forty-second Street subway stop at the Port Authority Bus Terminal. A calm night, lots of people about.

"Cocaine?" somebody called to me from a doorway.

I strode on briskly. My stride said that I was young, and not to be messed with, I thought. He had to be talking to one of the slower tourists around me. I doubled the purpose in my stride.

Suddenly they were on both sides of me, two of them, one at each elbow. "Cocaine, cocaine? Want cocaine, mister?" They grabbed my elbows and propelled me down the street into the light of a restaurant window.

One spun me out to face the street, locked my neck in a choke hold, and slammed my head against the window behind him.

Silence.

People gathered to stare.

While he slammed my head again and again on the window, his partner dug into my pants pockets. My wallet was in my upper left coat pocket, buttoned. Since I couldn't breathe or talk, I pointed to the coat pocket, trying to be helpful.

He ripped out the wallet and discovered my credit cards and seven dollars.

"No good! No good!" He waved the seven dollars in my face.

They thought about it. "Very bad. We got to do something about this."

Then his tone changed. "OK, OK, you can have these back." He stuffed the money and cards back into the wallet but before he could jam the wallet in my pocket, he and his pal were surrounded by six cops, four in plain clothes, all with guns pointed.

The choke-hold guy was spread-eagled against the window by a black cop who smashed his forehead against the glass. "That hurts!" he complained. The cop smashed his head again.

The two of them were handcuffed and hustled into the back of a beat-up undercover Plymouth that had just arrived at the corner with the plainclothes cops.

The uniformed cop and his partner had been dining inside the restaurant and noticed my head smashing into the window over their chops. That annoyed them.

In two minutes it was over.

One cop showed me a knife with a foot-long blade that had been hidden in the choker's boot and probably meant for my throat a few seconds later.

Transformed from victim to overlord with my own army, I confronted the guys in the back of the Plymouth, croaked out a demand that they remove their sunglasses and stared at them both, memorizing their features for later ID purposes, as I'd seen in TV movies.

I answered a few questions for the cops, donated five dollars to them as "evidence" of what was stolen and walked victorious, throat unslashed, through the curious crowd.

I hailed a downtown taxi and rasped to the cabbie that I only had two dollars for the fare, having just been mugged, but could we go to the Lion's Head Bar on Sheridan Square. Somebody there might lend me the rest of the fare. Surprisingly, he did not throw me out.

The cabbie waited outside the bar. Inside, one patron nursed a beer—Wilfrid Sheed, novelist, critic, last seen as I staggered through the *Whistle* party. He came up with the fare.

Alone with Sheed at the bar, I hoarsely described what had just happened. Sheed and I mused about where evil originated and he reminisced about raising children. He said that of all the children he and his wife, Miriam Ungerer, had raised together, the most toughly disciplined kids turned out the best. One answer to evil, I proposed, was disciplining kids. But what did I know? I had no kids.

Attempting again a strong youthful stride, I wobbled back to Bleecker Street. But I knew my youth and my stride wouldn't protect me in this city anymore. Perhaps I had always walked like an easy mark, a friendly guy who wouldn't struggle but would point to the pocket where his wallet might be found; the kind of guy who felt sorry for his muggers, so stupid that they attacked on a crowded, cop-ridden street and dragged me from the shadows into the light, and wasted seconds philosophizing about my mere seven dollars and what to do about the insult. They were stupid, or crazy.

Six blocks north of this spot at noon, a mugger had slashed a woman's throat when she refused to release her handbag. She died on the sidewalk in the mess of her own blood, while people on their lunch hours gawked.

Stupid, or crazy. It made no difference now.

It was time to move. New York cramped me with horror, with crowds.

It was time to move to a place where I could actually move.

For exercise, I pedaled daily on a stationary bike in front of a mirror at the local Apple Spa. I pedaled to nowhere, next to other bicyclers pedaling to nowhere and studying themselves in the same mirror. We pedaled so that we could continue to drink, smoke dope, and fuck, so that we could stay healthy enough and look good enough to do that.

Long ago I had resolved never to get near New York. It was the center of middlemen, hustlers, compromisers, and—worst of the lot—publishers.

Publishers, I declared, trade with words, and corrupt truth, for profit. I wanted nothing to do with them.

At nineteen, I had planned to astound the world with my first novel, untainted by commerce, announcing a truth that nobody had the nerve to experience or even think before.

I went to Paris and starved in an attic room, as legends had before me. Broke and back home, for years I wrote and rewrote that novel and endured rejection by contemptible publishers. I wrote other novels, all rejected. Too long out in the cold with my honest effort, I was losing my spirit in booze and depression.

I published my favorite novel myself, with an uncle's help. I became my own middleman, a publisher of last resort. A contemptible.

In my slow slide to compromise, I even joined Doubleday and then Putnam as an editor. But I was quickly found out, an author in disguise, and fired from both jobs.

On the outside again, I rededicated myself to honest labors. I published my *Pushcart Prize* collections in the guts of the commercial beast. Lots of good people were sympathetic and helped out as founding editors: Buckminster Fuller, Joyce Carol Oates, Ishmael Reed, Leslie Fiedler, Paul Bowles, Ralph Ellison, Reynolds Price—the masthead was a who's-who of integrity. *Publishers Weekly* gave the press its Carey-Thomas Award for creative publishing. Avon did the paperbacks of the *Pushcart Prize* and honored Pushcart at a Park Avenue dinner. Pushcart had promoted dozens of previously unknown writers.

The beast had been kind to me. But now it was time to leave. All I remembered of my years there was sex, food, and booze.

For Annie too, it was time to leave.

As a girl in Holly Springs, Mississippi, Annie had envisioned

New York as the city of El Morocco, just like in the movies. All the women were glamorous and lived in apartments where doormen announced gentlemen callers.

To Annie, New York was also a promise—if you went there you became a star. This was New York's contract with America.

Annie was seventeen when she enrolled at Finch College on East Seventy-seventh Street in 1964. Finch was a finishing school. Here you learned manners and how to speak without a Mississippi accent.

Within hours of Annie's arrival, New York started to keep its promise. She was invited to a real Cocktail Party at a Penthouse. They served mixed drinks and Annie wore a black cocktail dress with her beehive hairdo and she flirted with men, real men of twenty-five. No more swilling bourbon and necking with neighborhood boys in Holly Springs backseats.

After Finch, Annie left New York for two years at Northwestern University acting school. She was graduated first in her class, the same position as Ann-Margret the year before. But Annie was a dreamer, not a careerist. Turning up for auditions in New York seemed like work. Even if called back for a part, she seldom turned up. Annie hated to finish anything.

Annie liked to dream up projects and forget them. She lived to party, laugh, tell stories, and make new friends to tell about her imaginary projects.

One party's dream was Supergirls, a women-founded, women-run, women-staffed business that helped people with any problem or situation. Annie loved to help out.

Her more practical friend, Jessie, liked the idea and didn't let it evaporate with the rest of Annie's visions. They printed five hundred flyers announcing the Supergirls business and mailed them to Upper-East-Side addresses culled from the Celebrity Register. The phone rang once: Mrs. Cleveland Amory was gathering a scrapbook of puppy photos for her husband's birthday. Would the Supergirls follow her around with her new Siberian huskies, Ivan and Peter, and record their daily adventures? Annie and Jessie said they would.

Soon after, Annie sat down at dinner next to Howard Smith, a *Village Voice* columnist. He asked her what she did and she told him about Supergirls. He mentioned her dream in his next column.

In the months ahead, the phone rang a few more times. Business picked up. *Look* magazine wanted to do a feature. When Annie explained they had no office, and only a few clients, *Look* said they'd fake the whole layout with a borrowed office and models as clients. A three-page spread.

Johnny Carson's show called.

An NBC chauffeur picked up Annie and Jessie for a quick trip to Bloomingdale's to buy an outfit. Annie selected an electric green miniskirt.

Then there was the pre-interview, and the next night Annie was sitting next to Johnny while millions of Americans met twenty-four-year-old Annie McCoy, Supergirl, from Holly Springs, Mississippi.

Johnny seemed fascinated. He said she was "guileless." He held Annie and Jessie over for two segments while Pete Seeger and Peggy Cass paced in the Green Room.

Danielle Steele saw Annie on the Carson show and, before she had written her first novel, joined her as a Supergirl. A tiny dynamo, Annie remembered.

Annie, Jessie, and Danielle were the hit of the advertising business. They staged exhibitions and dinners for agency clients. Supergirls peddled Eve cigarettes—the first ever female cigarette—on street corners. Then, they considered it a breakthrough for women's rights. They designed home meditation centers, refurbished private yachts, and uncovered a long-abandoned subway stop below Grand Central Station for a theater party.

Supergirls opened branches in Washington and Atlanta. The "Charlie's Angels" TV show was inspired by their chutzpa.

But in a few years, the nation, corrupted by commercial sex, didn't even know the meaning of "guileless." It was widely assumed that Supergirls just had to be a call-girl ring.

As the business faded, Annie dreamed on. "I was a happy,

sunny puppy dog," she remembered. She and Jessie wrote an autobiography of Supergirls for Harper and Row, and a woman's guide to starting a business for Holt.

But while Annie daydreamed and told stories to her friends, many of them were leaving town for careers and marriage.

Only her Holly Springs friend, Pam, dreamed on with her. Now, instead of Nancy Drew fantasies in the streets of Holly Springs, Pam and her husband, Rod, planned to be the first to cross the Atlantic Ocean in a balloon—*The Free Life*. In the age of Vietnam, dropping out, and race riots, Pam, Rodney, and Annie drifted back to the nineteenth century with their balloon vision.

They read ballooning books, invested Rod's money in equipment, and hired an experienced British pilot. After three years of planning they were ready.

Annie waved good-bye as *The Free Life* and her best friend ascended into the clear skies of eastern Long Island on September 20, 1970, and headed off northward across Long Island Sound.

Twenty-eight hours later, the balloon's pilot radioed the Coast Guard that they were caught in a freak storm off Newfoundland and descending fast.

Annie, with Pam's father and a Coast Guard crew, searched the North Atlantic by air for two weeks. *The Free Life* left no trace.

"What could have gone wrong?" she remembered. "The ocean was a friend to Pam and me. We had played next to it on the sand. Death was just not an option."

Annie consulted a psychic who said that Pam was alive on an island in the far north. Annie hoped this was true and that any day Pam would call her to say she was OK, or that she would visit her in a dream, as Pam had promised. Annie longed for Pam's ghost to keep that promise.

When I met Annie at the *Whistle* party, New York was finished for her. Few friends were left to listen to her visions. The friends had become serious sorts with work to do.

Annie hated to be serious, almost as much as she disliked ordinary work.

Sophie

Annie was living out of a suitcase and lecturing at Union Dime banks on how women could start a business and get their life in order. "For Women Who Mean Business," the newspaper ads announced, "Annie McCoy, noted author, will deliver a series of six lectures." Annie was to have been paid $1,000 a lecture, but she never made it to the first one. She faked a fall down a subway stairway and called in to the bank with "a broken arm." The bank canceled the contract.

People stopped her on the street and asked for her autograph. She was tired of explaining that she was not Ellen Burstyn. She signed Burstyn's name on anything just to escape.

Soon after Ellen Burstyn won the Academy Award for *Resurrection*, a guy cornered Annie in a phone booth. He had to tell how her role in *Resurrection* had changed his life. "'Love really is everything,' like the movie said," he stood in the doorway and cried, while Annie listened, thanked him for the compliment, and waited for him to leave. He wouldn't. She slithered past him and bolted down the street.

Recently, a cab driver had told her that he recognized her as Ellen Burstyn. When she explained that she actually was not, he locked the doors and yelled, "You're not getting out of this cab until you admit who you are!" She confessed that he was right.

"I don't like being played for a patsy," he said.

Annie said she was sorry and she'd send him a signed photo of herself.

How could she tell him she was only the would-be author of a book about bananas? Banana history, banana menus, banana growing, banana economics, banana jokes? *The Complete Banana Book*. How could she explain that she had spent the advance and that she hadn't written word one about bananas?

Annie came to New York to dream. Now others dreamed her as somebody else.

I came to New York as a compromise.

For both of us it was over.

My mother had willed me enough money for a small house, shelter I could no longer afford in New York. In Wading River, far out on Long Island, I could bicycle to the post office, bicycle to the market, bicycle to the beach, bicycle to somewhere.

Annie and I didn't call it marriage. We didn't call it anything. We hardly knew each other.

In May 1981, we packed our few things into a small U-Haul truck and headed east down the Long Island Expressway to Wading River.

Waiting for us was a dinky, dark summer cottage with bunk beds in two small bedrooms and a huge plywood bar that took up most of the kitchen. Annie swore she'd never live there but we had no choice. It was all I could afford.

The land around it was as spectacular as the house was ordinary. The beach was a short walk down a dirt road, and on days with a northwest wind, the surf roared onto the sand and the bell buoy clanged. Through the budding trees we could see Long Island Sound, the same water that *The Free Life* had sailed over a decade ago. We planned to become strong riding our bikes through these woods and swimming in the sound.

As we drove that last mile to the house, leaving New York forever, we passed under a bower of just-blooming dogwood blossoms. Since colonial days, this area had been woodlots for the village. They harvested only the hardwoods and left the dogwoods. At this time of year, before the leaves were out, the pink and white blossoms formed a flowered path for our arrival.

I parked the U-Haul on the sandy driveway and we began carrying out enough gear to last our first night. Annie stuck a bottle of champagne in the refrigerator for a toast.

I was standing at the back of the truck in the twilight when I saw a figure stalking through the dogwoods toward me. He had no reason to be there, but this was the crime-free sticks and I wasn't concerned. Probably a neighbor dropping by to say welcome.

With him were two German shepherds, yanking at their leashes. When they spotted me, they began to howl. Under his arm he cradled a shotgun.

He halted a few feet away, barely keeping the dogs from me. "What do you think you're doing?" he demanded.

Annie came out of the house.

"What's in the truck?" he asked her.

She told him it was our furniture, and we had just arrived from the city. We would live here.

"We have a rapist on the loose. He just attacked a lady at the beach."

With that he headed back into the night. I never learned if he was a cop or just a civilian on posse patrol.

Quietly, we drank champagne.

That night we left the outside spotlight on and slept very little. We resolved to get a dog.

We named our dog Ellen Burstyn.

She was a young Chesapeake retriever mixed with something neurotic—a bounding black, hand-chewing, skinny, unfencible riot of flipped-out energy. She was totally useless as a guard dog. In fact, Ellen had no uses whatsoever.

To calm her down, we adopted Rocky. The people at the pound said he was "a Norman Rockwell," typical of the dogs in Rockwell's paintings. Rocky was everything that Ellen was not—calm, obedient, polite, short, plump, a gentleman—a world-class mutt.

Ellen and Rocky roamed the neighborhood as pals. They were welcomed, fed snacks, and petted because there was no harm in them. They chased no cats, barked at no cars.

They were our children.

Like parents, we worried when they didn't return home one evening. They were always in the house by dark, had never missed a night.

We advertised in the classified section of the local paper. "Dogs missing . . ." We posted the village and the woods with signs offering a fifty-dollar reward for information or sightings of the dogs. Kids called, hoping for the fifty dollars. "I saw a black dog around here yesterday . . ." but it was never Ellen or Rocky.

Annie and I borrowed a bullhorn and drove through the woods. "Rocky, Ellen. We're here . . ." Annie called out of the car window. But it was like her search for Pam in the North Atlantic. Nothing remained then—not a life jacket or strip of balloon. Nothing. Not a shred of response now, either. Her words traveled through the brown, empty woods and didn't stir the dogs where they floated in the new, unfenced pool of a developer's all-white, high-tech spec house.

We searched the state park nearby and asked the ranger if he had seen Rocky or Ellen. He hadn't, but we noticed five newborn white Labrador puppies penned outside his office. They were round and they were tripping over themselves to greet us.

A real estate agent found the dogs. She was showing the spec house to clients and discovered Rocky and Ellen drifting. She telephoned the dog warden and he told me where they were, just a half-mile from our house. A tarpaulin covering the pool had given way beneath them. I pulled them out of the cold water and laid them side by side on the deck scarred by their claws as they tried to struggle out. The dog warden assured me "they didn't suffer much," but the clawed wood told me everything.

Annie and I buried them under a hurricane-blasted oak in the backyard.

Then we cried.

I cried out of control with grief and nearly berserk with rage at the speculating house developer. I planned to burn his house down.

For Annie, it was worse. Her father had died in her arms less than a month before. At seventy-two years old, he had just returned home to Holly Springs after trying to lose weight quickly at a clinic. He was also escaping his alcoholic wife, and barely disguising suicide by starvation.

Annie had held him in her arms while blood poured from his bowels into the toilet.

As a doctor, he knew what was happening. A massive internal hemorrhage. But he didn't want her to call for help. "Sit me on the couch," he said. "You stay here and don't leave me."

He was very clear.

Annie did as she was told.

She watched him turn bone white, heard his death rattle. She ran to get her sleeping mother in the next room. He looked at both of them brightly and died.

Annie had not been able to cry then, nor at his funeral.

When Ellen and Rocky died, she sobbed for the dogs and for her daddy and would not get up.

I didn't know what to do for Annie. Then I remembered the puppies in the park. I told her I was going to have a look at them. She refused to let me take my wallet—if I bought a dog we might have to go through all this dying again, she said. I handed her my wallet, but slipped a check in my back pocket.

When I returned, the Labrador puppy sat in my palm, all tongue and wiggle. Annie took the puppy into her arms and laughed.

We named her Sophie, because she was as soft and over-stuffed as a sofa. Her newborn joy made our sorrow seem like bad manners.

Sophie slept at the foot of our bed, like Ellen and Rocky before her. She roamed the neighborhood, swam in the sound, lost her puppy fat, and grew large.

The veterinarian told us that many people spayed their females after six months. Otherwise, they would go into heat and howl and tear up the rug and draw males who would sit outside waiting, snarling, and crapping.

Most people thought that situation was inconvenient, he said.

One cold October morning, I walked into the bedroom where Sophie slept on her spot on the bed and fastened a leash to her neck. She thumped her tail and licked my hand, thinking a walk was coming up.

I was hung over, grumpy, and loose of tongue from yet another of the dinner parties that we and our friends gave for each other in constant rounds. We were all childless couples. A new country emptiness had replaced the free fucking nothingness of the city. I saw myself slumping into middle age, publishing one book after another, creeping to the end. A spirit was leaving my noncommercial cathedral.

Annie's dinner-table stories enthralled us still. Over and over, by our request, she repeated the story of her night on the "Tonight Show." Most of us seldom watched the show and thought of it—if we considered it at all—as the domain of fly-by-night celebrity. But we were fascinated by Annie's retelling. If we pleaded, and Annie was in the mood, she again became a guileless, gleeful girl of twenty-four.

That day, June 16, 1968, was an all-day deluge. "It pours with rain," as Annie put it.

"They take us right into makeup and slather us with pancake, powder, eye goo, lipstick, and rouge. We look like two dolls. Then they trot us to the Green Room, a shabby little place with two brown sofas, a monitor, a coffee machine, and a water-cooler. My stomach is a bottomless pit, filled with raw nerves, a million worms. I think I might have to pee but I can't be sure. My body doesn't belong to me any more. My hands don't look like my own hands, my feet aren't my own feet, I can't breathe. I can't talk to Jessie or Pete Seeger or Peggy Cass there next to me. I'm in total panic. Total.

"Suddenly the door swings open. This little guy sticks his head in. 'OK, who are the Supergirls?' he yells. I raise my hand. 'You're next. Three minutes. This way.' We follow the little guy out of the Green Room to behind these backstage curtains. We hear Johnny on the other side of the curtains doing his monologue. We follow the guy over a mess of tangled wires—it's a dump back there. Now we are one curtain away from Johnny. I'm supposed to be out first and sit next to Johnny. 'I'm going to be sick,' I say.

" 'Not here you're not. I'm not going out there alone. If you throw up, do it out there,' Jessie says.

"The curtain starts to move. The little man's hand is on my

elbow. He shoves me onto the stage. Actually shoves me out. I'm blinded by the spotlights. It's like walking into the sun. I can't see the audience. I turn. There's Ed, and then I see Johnny. We look at each other. I know then it's going to be OK. And it is."

The dinner guests want to know more.

"Johnny was kind, professional. He cared for us. I wasn't nervous anymore. He knew the script and fed it to us. After the commercial break, I stood to leave, but he said, 'Naa, naa, naa, please stay. Sit down.' He said we were naturals, refreshing. We stayed for another segment. Then he wished us a long run and great success and told the audience to give us a big hand and we left. I felt like I'd fallen off a cliff, it was so hard to come down from that high."

More questions from the dinner guests. Did Johnny smirk about Supergirls as an escort service?

"We were plucky kids, starting a business when women usually didn't do that. He admired us. That's all," Annie said.

It was Annie's most popular story, topping even her retelling of the *Free Life* tragedy and her hunt for the balloon for two weeks over the North Atlantic in the company of horny coast guardsmen and her many tales about Holly Springs, Mississippi.

But dinner-table stories alone wouldn't relieve our everyday sterility. Annie and I were locked in a dull pattern in a shoddy bungalow.

That morning, hung over again, I snapped Sophie's leash on her collar.

"Come on, Sophie. Let's get sterile, like everybody else," I snarled. "Sterile is in this year."

Annie and I looked at each other, startled at what I had just revealed.

That night, while Sophie recuperated from her operation at the animal hospital, I dreamed I was holding my just-born child in my arms. A great white light shone around my child and me. I said in my dream, "This is what it is all for."

In ecstasy, I woke up.

Annie woke at the same moment. "I was just dreaming," she said. "Maybe we could adopt a baby from Peru."

It seemed the only way. Annie was past forty by now. And she lacked an ovary, removed years ago in an operation for a benign cyst.

We hugged each other and slept.

6

Plastic Cup

AS A CHILD, Annie's mother had lived in an antebellum mansion overlooking Charlottesville, Virginia. Her mom's dad was a vice president of the Southern Railroad and a pal of Enrico Caruso. Her dad reserved a private car for Caruso, and the family and Caruso rode up and down the South coast enveloped in Caruso's singing. Often Caruso visited the mansion on the hill, and the halls echoed with his voice, or so it seemed in her mother's Heaven Hill bourbon memories.

Later, alone in her Holly Springs apartment while her husband worked at the hospital, Annie's mom drank Heaven Hill from waking to sleeping. She sometimes fell, broke bones, and cut herself. Dr. McCoy would call Annie to fly down from New York and nurse her mother. When Annie asked her mother why she drank, she would only shake her head rapidly and cry.

Before her marriage she had been a teetotaler.

Annie's sister, Beatrice, found her mother's romantic mansion again. She had married an Englishman with a castle in the Cotswolds. Lady Bea lived within the walls and towers of Henry VIII's last wife, Catherine Parr. She commanded a staff of fifty who addressed her as "your ladyship." Only Caruso was lacking.

Annie had ended up in my summer shack.

To me, a house was something to keep the rain off and the cold out. A tent would do almost as well. The dwelling was not important as long as you lived a worthy life inside it. Worthy meant thinking, writing, and publishing inspired words. Words like the Bible was alleged to contain. A house was useful only in keeping the writers and publishers of words warm and the paper dry.

A house might have other minor uses, too: as an investment, for instance, the only investment I would ever make, thanks to my mother's dying gift. But otherwise, a house meant bills for improvements, repairs, and taxes.

To me, money was a virus. Money could make you sick. Worse, money corrupted words. To make money, writers twisted words and publishers lied about the twistings.

Much worse, for want of money, I might have to go get a daily job.

To Annie, a house was at least half of us.

That half died when she painted the inside of the back door white.

I told her I wished she had at least consulted me about the white door. I wanted to leave it bare wood.

"This is my house, too!" she blindsided me. I was two beers into a lovely Sunday lunch at a Riverhead restaurant and I wasn't ready for this. I hadn't yet realized her family passion for houses.

"How did I ever get from Mississippi to New York to that loathsome house? What am I doing out here? This isn't any fun!" Annie hollered, rising to her full theatrical talent. People were looking at us.

"I didn't say you couldn't paint the door white. I only wish you had asked me first."

"I'm sick of it all. That's a horrible house."

"OK, you can have your white door."

"It's my house, too!"

"Of course. Just ask next time you paint."

"I want another house."

But there was nothing I could do for Annie. I would not sell my first and perhaps only house.

With a small inheritance from her father, Annie began hunting for her own house. She invited me to rent the bungalow and join her, but things had gotten so shaky between us that I said no.

As our second Wading River winter started and Annie's forty-first birthday neared, we talked not at all about adopting a Peruvian child, and more and more about Annie moving out.

Still, Annie cooked with ceremony. No dinner was ever thrown on the table. She dipped into her inheritance and devoted entire afternoons readying her daily food events from scratch. In our shack, we ate castle chow. Annie's seafood pasta, Annie's own shepherd pie. Annie's special meat loaf, Annie's stuffed game hen, Annie's three-day-marinated filet mignon.

Such devotion to my dinner confused and lulled me. If she loved what I ate, did she perhaps still love me? I was ready for another blindsiding.

"In one day I can love you and hate you," Annie began, over our second bottle of red wine at dinner. "But today I finally decided. It's over. I'm leaving. Finished!"

She was suddenly screaming.

Sophie hid behind the couch.

"Every night you're off to the bar for your drink and I stay home and cook. We do nothing together. Nothing. You go out and have affairs. You ignore me. I left my friends in New York for you and now I am totally alone in this loathsome place."

Loathsome was one of Annie's favorite words. She strung out the *loo*.

Stilled by the food and wine, I had no reply. I nodded and drank, silenced by the word *affairs*.

I didn't know how she had guessed about the other girl, but since she took an affair for granted, I didn't act innocent.

Her name was Margot Kim, a poet-photographer, twenty-five, part Korean, part French. At a Boston street fair, she had stopped at my bookselling booth and said, "I'm interested in you."

At a pub nearby, I had told her about Annie, and our dogs drowning, and the white door, and what a great cook Annie was, and about how she had been a hit on TV and about her friend who tried to balloon across the Atlantic, and how we were thinking of having children, but we didn't have much time left because of Annie's biological clock and the one-ovary thing, and maybe we would adopt a baby, and Annie was just not destined to be a mother of children probably because if she had been she would have been married by now or tried harder to have children by now, about how Annie was an actress, first in her class, and a romantic, and a comedian, and a terrific friend and mistress, but no mother, and even if she was, there might be defects in the baby at her age, and she constantly says she loves me, then wants to leave . . .

Margot smiled and nodded.

"I want to go to bed with you," she said.

I followed her upstairs to her hotel room.

"This is just for laughs, right?" I asked her. "I don't want to mislead you. I think Annie is my woman."

In the morning I told her more about Annie.

Annie went back to New York to check out an apartment for herself on Prince Street. While she was there, she had lunch with Timmie, an ex-Supergirl who had just had a baby boy at thirty-nine. Timmie brought the baby along and he slept in a basket on the table between them.

Annie told Timmie about her great fall from New York to a shack in the woods. She said she was probably leaving the shack, but didn't know where to go. All her friends had left New York. She told Timmie about adopting a Peruvian child, or even having one of our own, but it was probably too late . . .

"Do it!" Timmie interrupted, and banged her hand on the table.

The baby woke up.

"I'm too old. I've got one ovary left. There are too many tests," Annie said.

"Do it! Get the tests. Do everything! You haven't got a whole lot of time!"

"The tests hurt . . ."

"Yes, they do hurt. They hurt a lot. So what!"

The baby started to cry. Timmie lifted him from the basket and handed him to Annie. He calmed down, stopped crying.

"Children are the only thing in the world," Timmie told Annie. "The only thing."

That night at the bungalow, Annie prepared her seafood pasta— mussels, shrimp, scallops, cubes of monkfish in her own red sauce. She told me about the crummy apartment she saw on Prince Street and her lunch with Timmie.

"My ears opened up today," she said. "I'm going for the tests." We clinked glasses.

That night I dreamed that I visited my father. He lived alone in a rooming house. Pop told me that Mom had left him and taken the kids. He said in the dream that he no longer believed in Jesus. There could be no God in a world where people hurt other people so badly. Pop sat on the side of the bed, his face in his hands, totally alone, destroyed by a woman's disloyalty.

When we woke in the morning, Annie announced that she had changed her mind. There would be no tests after all. No kid.

"I don't feel good about you when I think of you as the father of my child. I like you better when I don't think of you as a father," she concluded.

I sat on the side of the bed and agreed with her. "We'd probably just end up as two fat old drunks," I said. "Booze in your family. My granddad a drunk, too. If we had a kid, we'd just have to stay together to the losing end, two old drunks. The kid would get the genes and be a drunk, too."

"Plus we'd be over sixty when the kid is twenty."

I nodded. "First you want the kid and I don't. Then I want the kid and you don't. First we adopt and then we don't adopt. This is the first time we both agree. No kid."

"No kid."

At nine o'clock that morning, Dr. Carol Livoti, the baby doctor, called from New York to confirm the appointment Annie had made from a pay phone after her lunch with Timmie. Dr. Livoti was an Italian mama gone undercover as a practitioner of medicine.

Annie was just about to announce her no-kid, no-test verdict when Dr. Livoti broke in: "And don't worry about that one-ovary stuff. You can have a baby with half an ovary. Be here next Wednesday so we can do an exam and set up the tests. And hurry. Time's wasting."

Because Annie was going to the city anyway on another apartment hunt, she agreed to drop by and see Dr. Livoti.

At her office, Dr. Livoti did a basic exam and pronounced Annie fit for childbearing. Her tests would begin in two weeks.

But I was the first question.

She handed Annie a plastic cup.

"We test him first. Then we test you. Tell him not to dawdle. The sperm goes in this cup and real quick the cup goes to this laboratory." She scribbled the New York address of the lab.

"I will let you know what they report about Bill's sperm the minute they call me."

When Annie told me about the sperm test, I remarked that this would be the first test I'd actually enjoy. I took the bus to New York, the cup in my pocket.

I'd deposit the sperm in the cup in the men's room of the YMHA, then rush it to the lab down the road. But how would I explain to the guard why I needed the use of the men's room? "I want to have a child? My girlfriend's doctor wants a test of my sperm. I'm from out of town and I have to use your bathroom because I have to get to the lab fast."

Too complicated.

So I imitated a student, some Pushcart books under my left arm—*The Art of Literary Publishing* and *The Little Magazine in America* —the cup in my right-hand pocket. But I was too old for this milling crowd of Y kids. The guard might spot my fakery. I worried about this while trying to protect the plastic cup from being smashed by the bumping kids.

The cup was wrapped in a scrap of *Screw* magazine featuring photos of a couple deep into fellatio and humping, photos meant to get me terribly excited and deliver to Dr. Livoti a full measure of industrious sperm.

I had only a half hour to get the sperm from Ninety-second Street to the laboratory on Seventy-eighth Street. After that I figured the sperm would begin dying and I'd flunk my sperm test. But first I had to get past this guard.

I knew the territory.

A few years ago, Robert Lowell had read here and I had brought a date to listen.

I knew the history.

This was the evening literary center of New York. Truman Capote had made his debut here in 1949, in a black velvet suit, fortified with brandy, and he had returned to encore after encore. They had to flick the house lights to get Truman off the stage. Dorothy Parker had recited here, a bit tipsy, and after the applause she had seemed to forget that she had already read. She had started her program again, and had been gently escorted away. Dylan Thomas had read four voices from *Under Milk Wood* here, just a few days before he died.

The world's literary greats had spoken here, and perhaps a few had used the toilet I was now reconnoitering.

Not only was I guilty of impersonating a student and unable to explain why I was here, I was also about to commit the Old Testament sin of Onan at the Young Men's Hebrew Association.

As a boy I had not practiced this sin. I'd known nothing about it. Such things were not mentioned at home. I heard about "beating your meat" on the playground but hadn't had the nerve to ask what that meant. I'd found out by accident, fiddling with my-self, quite late, at sixteen. I'd done a lot of praying for forgiveness in the years after.

I studied the guard from a corner just inside the street door for so long that I worried he might feel my eyes on him.

I walked back into the street, waited a minute, then rushed back into the Y, past the guard, toward the men's room as if I were in such a hurry that he'd better not mess with me or we might have an accident on the floor.

I made it.

This was one of the finer men's rooms, with mirrors, urinals, and many stalls. And empty, too. I might be able to fill the cup with hot sperm and enjoy myself in this comfortable place . . . im-portant to enjoy it, or the sperm count might be low.

I selected a stall at the end of the row, away from the door, against a wall. If somebody sat down in the stall next to me, there would be nobody on the other side. But who would sit down next to me, with an entire range of empty stalls?

I hung my army coat—Annie's dad's World War II coat—on the inside of the door and dropped my jeans on the floor, to ap-pear as if on normal business to an observer from outside.

I got to work.

In my left hand was the scrap of *Screw* photos. In my right hand, my moistened instrument. The cup was on the floor until needed.

I was well along, marveling at the fellatio and the doggie-humping, when I reached for the cup and realized that this was going to be impossible to do sitting on a toilet. The cock was straight up. The cup had to get under it. That meant standing. But if I stood up, head above the door, an intruder might wonder about my purposes and interrupt my concentration.

I tried it anyway. I placed my *Screw* scrap on the seat. I was again reaching for my cup, when the men's room door banged open and someone headed for the stall right next to me.

I grabbed the *Screw* photos and sat down. The cock deflated.

From the other stall, silence. He had not even dropped his pants. I waited, scrap in hand.

Ignoring the strange silence next to me, I continued as quietly as I could. This would not be a wild, relaxed, fully-committed event, but it would have to do.

If I could not stand up and position the cup, it might work horizontally. I propped my feet on the stall door, sliding down on the seat, careful not to slide off entirely.

A horrible moaning from next door. A crazy moaning.

Maybe the guy broke up with his girl, I thought. I hoped he'd get over whatever it was and leave soon, or maybe he would climb or crawl into my stall. And still his pants had not hit the floor. He was approaching a wail.

The guard would be in here pronto to check on the problem.

I worked quickly, horizontal on the seat. The *Screw* clipping fluttered out of my hand and I snatched the cup, managing to catch most of what feebly emerged.

I capped the cup and shoved it back into the army coat pocket. I rushed out of the stall, past the incoming guard, into the hall, leaving the photos and the books behind.

On windy Madison Avenue, the temperature was in the teens. The sperms might already be expiring in the cold.

I figured that in the traffic, running would be just as fast as a cab. Ignoring red lights, daring cars to bother with me, I dashed south.

Optilabs was a walkdown storefront, a small room with a counter and a young nurse behind it. Several patients sat on metal folding chairs, waiting to be tested.

How to tell the nurse in front of these people that I had a cup of sperm in my pocket for her? There was no use pretending that this sperm got into this cup by any other way than it did.

She looked up at me.

I took the cup out of my pocket. "I have a sample for Dr. Carol Livoti."

"Yes." She checked her records. "Sperm. You must be Bill."

I handed her the cup.

"Sixteen dollars," she said.

I handed her a twenty and was hurrying out when she called, "Your change!"

I returned.

"What's your rush?" she smiled, placing four dollars in my hand.

I felt stickiness on her fingers.

"Wait," she ordered.

From a box under the counter, she produced a paper towel and divided a sheet. One for her. One for me.

"Good-bye," she smiled, cleaning her hands.

7

Anniversary

CAROL LIVOTI'S review was upbeat. "I want to hire that sperm! You next, Annie."

Annie reported to Livoti's New York office for her first test, a biopsy of the remaining ovary, a particularly nasty and embarrassing procedure, performed while she was spread on a table under bright lights, and a tiny man with stubby fingers, Livoti's designated assistant, fooled around with her insides. Later she remembered scalpels, knives, scissors, and the top of the man's bald head as he bent over her, poking, snipping, and saying nothing.

Dr. Livoti called the next day to announce that she had passed the test. The second test, a fallopian tube blowout, was set by Livoti for seven days later.

The day before the blowout, Annie and I talked it all over at lunch. "I only have one tube to do, so maybe it won't be too bad," she said, optimistically.

We ordered two turkey club sandwiches, stared out the window at the gray winter street, and fumbled for conversation.

As our sandwiches arrived, Annie said, "Are you intending to run away with Jimmy Swaggart?"

I had watched Swaggart on TV the evening before, fascinated by his talent and moved against my will.

"He's a great religious actor. That's all."

"You're not planning to run off with him?"

I shook my head, smiled.

"I don't want a religious nut as father to my child." She was working up to another blindsiding, mad about Swaggart, mad about the house, mad in general. "I don't know about the tube blowout. It's going to hurt. I'm so unhappy. I don't know where to go or how to start going there."

I told her a story, the history of Tad and Terry. When we were students in Paris in the early sixties and I was working on my first novel, Tad had gotten Terry pregnant. We were all broke and living together in a beat-up student hotel. He was black, she was English. They planned to go to Switzerland for an abortion. I hadn't wanted them to give up the baby so easily. I was fascinated by Faulkner in those days. I had grown a mustache, just like Faulkner's. I had told Tad and Terry the mustache was a Faulkner soul-mustache for their kid. As long as the kid grew in her, I would keep the mustache. If they killed the kid, I would shave it off and flush it down the toilet just like they did with their kid. They had canceled the abortion.

"So where's the kid now?" Annie asked skeptically.

"Terry miscarried in the hotel room. It all came out on copies of the *International Herald Tribune*."

I took out my wallet and showed her a 1964 photomat shot of myself with the Faulkner mustache.

"You look like a Bulgarian assassin," Annie scoffed.

She was right. I looked nothing like Faulkner.

"I'm not having this test. I don't want a baby. Tell me what to do. Please. I don't know what's going on."

That night, the weather report warned of near-blizzard conditions for the next day. It would probably be impossible to get to New York anyway.

Annie and I decided to let the weather decide for us.

The next day was frigid with a hazy sunrise.

Annie caught the first train to New York.

In Livoti's office, the little assistant with the stubby fingers blasted air through her one tube. Ready for pain, Annie later told me she felt almost nothing. A sharp, brief cramp.

Then she and the little man watched on a screen as dye flowed through the tube. The tube was clear.

Dr. Livoti was pleased. "There's nothing wrong with you. One more test to go."

Afterward, Annie visited a woman psychologist and asked for advice. She told her about the suspected other woman, about her loneliness while I had a drink at the pub each night and left her cooking, about the dinky house. The psychologist told Annie she could do anything she wanted to do. All Annie had to do was make up her mind what it was she wanted to do.

As she was riding back to Wading River on the train, the blizzard struck from the northeast with classic force. Ten inches of snow collected in an hour. By mid-Island, she could see nothing outside the window.

It was so bad by the time I arrived at the train station to meet her that I reserved a motel room in the village, uncertain whether we could drive the few miles back to the house.

The ticket agent told me that the Long Island Rail Road system was near collapse. Switches were frozen, signal lights out. The drifts piled halfway up the station wall. Annie's train was three hours late when I heard the whistle from the west and then saw dimly the train's headlights through the whiteout.

The train stopped. Forms struggled off.

I couldn't find her. "Annie!" I yelled into the blinding snow. "Over here! I'm down this way!"

I walked the length of the platform without finding her.

I started back. "Annie, Annie!" Perhaps she had missed the train.

Then from the other side of the station, I heard her calling my name. "Bill, where are you?"

We yelled and yelled and guided ourselves with our voices.

We ran to each other and hugged and kissed as if we had long been separated by continents.

Lovers again, holding hands, we slid and groped our way to a nearby bar.

Annie told me about her tube test, and what the psychologist said. "All I have to do is make up my mind."

"So?"

"On the train, I finally made up my mind," Annie said. "I'm going away by myself this summer. To Maine. I don't want any more tests. Kids make me nervous. I have to think about that."

"In Maine?"

"Yes. In Maine I will decide."

By the time we left the pub, the snow had stopped. The plows had cleared the road. Through the moon-bright snowfields we drove home in a night of extraordinary clarity.

Annie was a ceremonial woman.

Because the next week—February 22—was the anniversary of our meeting at the *Whistle* party, she bought a baguette, two bottles of fine Médoc, a vegetable pâté, and two brands of Pont L'Évèque, my favorite cheese. In a wicker basket, she placed two long-stemmed wine glasses, two Bibi pottery plates, a corkscrew, and a red and white checked tablecloth.

Our anniversary picnic.

At sundown, with Sophie in the back seat, we drove her dad's '78 Chevy Caprice to the nearby beach and stopped at the end of a road overlooking the ice-rimmed sound. The woods were dead, but now and then a blue jay squawked. Mating squirrels chased each other through the branches. In only a few weeks spring peepers would chorus and the crocuses would bloom.

Annie spread the tablecloth on the front seat between us. I uncorked a bottle and filled our glasses.

"To *Whistle*! To James Jones! To our five years!" I raised my glass to the gray sunset.

"Five years of putting up with Bill. And that's enough," Annie said.

"To the next fifty years!" I laughed.

Did she prepare this fancy ceremony to announce the end? I didn't want to lose her. Even in her confusion about me, she had been a friend. She was loyal to all her friends, sacrificed for them, for her booze-obliterated parents. But I was helpless to guide her.

"You don't even remember kissing me at the *Whistle* party," Annie said.

"Sure I do," I lied.

"You were smashed."

"I do recall kissing this blond vision. You, I presume. Then I kissed Ruth Carter Stapleton. That I am sure of. We wrote to each other before she died last year. Two letters."

"You remember the faith healer. Me, you forgot."

"I remember a good time. Plus an epiphany. Love is God."

"You're going to run off with Jimmy Swaggart."

"Who are you going to run off with?"

"I haven't decided yet. The first man that shows up."

I didn't know whether to believe her or not.

We finished the wine and most of the anniversary picnic. Sophie helped. We watched the last of the sun leave the ice.

"I'm going to a fat farm next month," she said.

"What fat farm?"

"I don't know yet. Upstate, maybe. For a few weeks."

"Good. When you get hard, I get hard." It was my dig about Annie's increasing plumpness and the waning of our passion.

She stared at me in the twilight.

"All men are from outer space," Annie pronounced. About this she was certain. Men were unfathomable and she had snagged herself the prime example.

It was cold. I started the car and we drove toward our hut.

"You know what the third test would have been?" Annie asked. "We go to Livoti's office and fuck in a room. We fuck all day and they check what happens inside me."

For our anniversary dinner, Annie had concocted a lamb stew. I opened another bottle of Médoc and waited at the dining room table, forbidden to help her, as always, in her careful preparation.

I had just salvaged the table from the town dump and I was proud of it. Most of our furniture came from the dump.

This table was Annie's writing desk during the day and it was piled with recent chapters of a novel she had worked on the past year with her friend, Paula. From my garage office I would hear them laughing about the adventures of their heroines.

Writing under the pseudonym of Georgia Hampton, they planned to knock off Danielle Steele as the most popular hack writer in the world. They would become incredibly rich. Then Annie could buy the house she coveted. And why not? What Danielle Steele did seemed very simple, easy to imitate and surpass. Besides, they remembered, Danielle Steele had once been a Supergirl, employed by Annie not much over a decade ago.

After a year of trying, and dozens of rejections, Annie and Paula still laughed through rewrite after rewrite, month after month, entertaining themselves with their entertainment.

Writing was supposed to be hard, I thought. When I wrote, when my friends wrote, agony was assumed to be a necessity. If it wasn't painful, it wasn't any good. From the hoots reaching me in my garage, I learned a new angle to writing—it could be fun.

At the table, waiting for my lamb stew, I read the synopsis and most recent draft for *Seductions*, finally sold the week before to a paperback division of Putnam. It was about Dahlia and Cassie, best friends and just graduated from Miss Bennett's Academy for Girls. "For them, the world was a confection of paradise—from all-night parties with champagne at dawn to the sun-studded beaches of the Riviera; from New York's gleaming towers of high finance to the sensuous romance of Paris. Life was a banquet . . .," the synopsis announced.

"Dahlia, born to wealth and class, leads a glittering life of casual affairs. Cassie, the poor relation of a well-to-do family, craves and wins success, riches and power. But is the sacrifice she has to make too great?"

While Annie spun the salad and heated the stew, I read the

first chapter. A Greek island in the Aegean. Two wealthy ladies, Cassie and Dahlia, strip and make love to each other on a rocky beach while a boy of eleven, also naked, watches from a crack in a rock cliff.

Annie and Paula had captured that Greek island perfectly. The sun, the sea, the oiled sex, the little boy spying on his first passion. They even spelled *bouzouki* right!

This was good stuff, certainly a step above hackwork, and far beyond Danielle Steele. It verged on literature, which was probably why it took the agent longer than a year to sell it.

"This is terrific!" I said, digging into the stew. "I thought you were just messing around all year. But this is good. Real good."

"Have another glass of wine."

"I mean it. The stew's not bad, either."

Annie said nothing.

She fed the leavings of the stew to Sophie while I flipped through her chapters.

I was falling in love all over again with this amazing woman. She was dreaming Greece for me, and Paris. And she was beautiful and funny and a fabulous cook.

Annie was silent.

She put the leftover salad away.

I restacked the *Seductions* chapters on the table, poured another glass of wine, and punched the TV on. I'd just had a fantastic revelation about Annie's genius.

I relaxed in my admiration.

Suddenly she was around the corner and in front of the set. She snapped it off.

"We have to talk," she announced.

"About what?" I smiled.

"Us."

"OK."

"We are breaking up."

"Really?" I was bewildered. And drunk. And helpless.

"Yes. Really!"

I sat in the chair while she banged around in the tiny bedroom, packing her things into two suitcases.

"You dragged me out here against my will! I am angry! Angry!" she shouted.

Sophie, terrified, scrambled into the bathroom, then back into the living room. She peed on the rug and headed back into the bathroom.

I stared at the puddle of pee.

"I used to wonder if you were the best thing to happen to me," Annie declaimed. "How could I have been so stupid! I am the best thing that ever happened to you. And you don't know that! You don't even see that!"

"Yes, I do. Tonight I do."

"Too fucking late!"

She slid the door open and threw her bags into the front seat of her father's Chevy.

She came back into the house for something. I stood and touched her arm. "Where are you going?"

"I don't know. I don't care. I am going!"

"Please do me one last favor?"

"What!" she screamed.

"Wait until morning. You can't drive around out there in the dark with no place to go."

I took the car keys from her hand.

"You can leave in the morning. I'll help you find a place to stay."

She ran into the bedroom.

I lay on the couch, sleepless.

About midnight, the phone rang.

It was Paul Rogers, just out of Sing Sing Prison, winner of my first annual Editor's Book Award for a manuscript overlooked by the greedy, compromising commercial publishers. His novel, *Saul's Book*, published by me that winter, detailed the homosexual rough-trade life he lived in Times Square. The *Village Voice* reviewer, Eliot Fremont Smith, had called it "one of the most repellent books I have ever read." He added that it was also a masterpiece.

Paul was on his good drugs. He felt fine.

"I'm sorry about the hour, Bill. I just wanted to say I love you for saving my novel and publishing it when all the shits wouldn't do it. I do love you, you know that?"

I said I did. I thanked him and hung up.

On other evenings, on his bad drugs, Paul had threatened to sue me, or worse, for imagined slights. At an editorial conference in his Queens apartment, he had stolen my Mastercharge card from the wallet in my jacket hanging over a chair, and then bought himself a stereo and two tickets to see Elizabeth Taylor at a Broadway show.

It was only two hours to my house from Times Square. I never knew what Paul would do, what drug he would be on. Recently I had kept a loaded shotgun in my office—packed with birdshot, since I didn't want to really hurt him. Only scare him if he showed up on his bad drugs.

Mostly, Paul didn't believe in my literary good works, or good works period. He respected clever ripoffs and "getting over" on saps and marks. His idea of sex was a few minutes of sadism or masochism—he didn't care which—with a stranger at the baths. Two years after this call, he would be murdered by his fourteen-year-old boyfriend as he lay drug-stupefied in bed.

Now I thought it was me he would murder.

I put the answering machine on.

Paul called back again and again through the night. Over and over he told me he loved me. He ran out the tape.

Annie slept through it.

I lay on the couch and watched the sky brighten over the sound. The birds were in full racket. A deer poked around the front yard.

Annie woke and headed into the kitchen. She cooked grits, once-over-lightly eggs, and Canadian bacon.

Without a word, she put it on the table in front of me.

"I decided not to go," she said.

"I think you should go, Annie. You have always wanted to leave. Your bags are packed. Go. Do it now."

She cried, helplessly.

I was seeing it her way, I thought. She was exactly who she envisioned she was—a woman of enormous talent and charm. Johnny Carson's guileless girl; the friend who went to the ends of the ocean to find Pam after the balloon wreck. A loyal, giving person; in fact, the only real Christian I had met besides Ruth Carter and my mother. But I was not worth the pain I gave her in return.

There had to be a better place for Annie than this shed. She deserved to recapture that Virginia mansion for her mother. She ought to be swept away in romance by a fellow just like Caruso. Maybe she would meet some rich guy south of the Montauk Highway on a Southampton estate.

All she got from me was furniture from the dump, and my headscratching bewilderment. A guy who thought money was germs.

She was on the wrong side of the highway.

If she migrated south and east toward the ocean, she'd save her life.

At ten o'clock, she left, sobbing.

I had no idea to where.

At noon, she called me from a motel, miles away. "Here I am. All alone. Just like Jean Harris. And all I ever wanted was for us to do things together."

Jean Harris, I recalled, had just shot her lover, the diet doctor. Annie revered Jean Harris.

8

Child

"HONEY, WE'RE GOING to have a baby!"

Margot Kim was calling from New London.

"A baby! Are you sure?"

She was sure.

The day before, she had let me know she was twelve days late and going for a test. We'd know at noon.

And such a March noon! The sun was hot, the snowdrops and crocuses were blooming, the spring peepers were cacophonous, and the children of all species were swarming to life.

I hugged Sophie, danced around the empty house, and packed a bag for a long weekend. Margot and I would celebrate our wonderful accident in the mountains. We'd escape to the Catskills and laugh and plan and name the kid.

I gave Sophie the run of the woods and rushed for an afternoon ferry across Long Island Sound to New London.

Annie had been holed up in her motel for three weeks, working on her novel, calling me now and then. "I just wanted to shake us up," she said. "Not break us up."

I thought I'd call Annie from New London and tell her about

Margot's baby. This was better for Annie. She'd find the right rich man now. I hoped she would see it like that.

Margot and I hadn't thought of doing it this way. We hadn't thought much at all. In fact, we didn't read the small print on the spermicide box that directed us to apply spermicide to the diaphragm before each occasion, not just once an evening. Our love affair had been a year-long series of restaurant chatter and one-night stands. Now, because we hadn't read the fine print, we were mom and pop to be.

Suddenly it was all certain. Here at last was the future. I celebrated the child and Margot and the end of ambiguity.

In New London, it was a clear spring twilight. Margot lived just up the hill from the harbor. I bought champagne at the liquor store and some Fritos and a bunch of tulips at the deli downstairs.

I charged up the three stone flights to Margot's basic, apprentice photographer/poet apartment, with the shower in the kitchen and the mattress on the floor.

We parents-to-be held each other and waltzed around the tiny kitchen, like all delirious parents-to-be before us. We sat on Margot's mattress and knocked back the champagne from paper cups and, slightly drunk, telephoned her friends with the news. A June wedding would be announced, we told them. It would be an amazing bash—for them, for us, for the new baby.

We stumbled down the stairs to the Golden Panda restaurant on the harbor, our rendezvous spot.

"Margot," I said across the table, "this looks like it might be getting serious . . ."

"Yes!" she cheered.

"Well, tell me about yourself. I mean tell me all about yourself. I need to know everything."

She looked at me, a question in her mind.

"I mean your past. Your parents. Family stuff. History."

She was silent.

"You are going to be my wife. I want to know everything about my wife."

"But you've known me for a year. Right . . . ?"

"Sure."

"I've already told you lots of that."

"I know. I know. But it's different now."

"You have been paying attention?" she asked.

"Of course."

We turned to our food.

What I knew about Margot so far was that after we met at the street fair in Boston, we had shacked up for two days and nights at the Copley Plaza on her daddy's credit card, and had never left the room.

This was fun, and simple, a game without complications.

When I reminded her about Annie and our confusions, she said it didn't matter. "I don't have any war with Annie. The war is over if you want it to be."

She had learned this slogan from her dad, a veteran of the South Korean Army, and presently security supervisor for a large Boston hospital. She and her dad were very close and often took handgun practice together at a shooting range near their suburban home. Her mom, a French citizen, lived most of the time in a small town outside of Paris.

According to Margot, this was going to be more laughs than sorrow or it was going to be nothing at all. "I'm your tart in training," she reminded me.

At the Boston hotel and on her New London mattress, Margot had worked me over with sensual skill and single-minded conviction and afterwards threw in a half-hour of Shiatsu. Then we smoked a joint and eased into our next bout of play.

Margot told me about her twenty-five years: two semesters at Bard College, her most recent job at a fancy Westport camera shop, her real love—writing poetry, which she refused to let me read.

I talked about my problem: needing women. A fixation of the mind and soul.

Margot said she understood.

"I feel sorry for all men," she said, rubbing my temples as I lay on the mattress between her knees.

I told her that last summer Annie had actually announced our wedding to her mother and the Southern relatives. Then Annie canceled it. No explanation.

"I feel sorry for you," said Margot.

We talked on the phone, through the year, about her cat, her photographs, her poetry—about Annie. She constantly photographed me and put the framed photos on top of her small piano, next to shots of Walt Whitman, Emily Dickinson, and Mark Strand. She played the piano with more determination than skill, twisting Mozart into a march.

We met at the wharf, we ate at the Golden Panda, screwed all night and, exhausted, I boarded the ferry in the morning for Long Island. Often the ferry would pass outbound nuclear subs leaving their base in the Groton Harbor across the Thames River.

I told Annie I had been in New York on business.

Once Margot and I had an entire weekend together, at a poetry conference she signed up for on Block Island. Between seminars we had biked around the island and marveled at a rainbow arching over the island, placed there just for us, we assumed. In our room overlooking the sea, Margot said she wanted little more in life than to be postmistress at a post office somewhere, to adore her kids, to write poems and snap photos.

I told her that I was terrified that Annie would become pregnant. She'd be a crazy mom. She had screamed at me all week, in top theatrical voice, about nothing, that I could figure out.

Margot was sorry.

In that rainbow afternoon, I thought Margot was bright, caring, pretty, smart, the sort of girl Mom would have liked.

Like Mom, she didn't seem to have her own agenda. No spectacular housing ambitions, no visions of transatlantic balloon flights, or knocking off Danielle Steele. Margot was a suburban woman and happy about it.

I was stuck between Annie and Margot. Immobilized.

Commuting back and forth on the ferry, I developed a hacking cough that wouldn't clear up. The doctor said my blood pressure was 170 over 110 and I needed beta blockers.

Margot said her uncle took blood pressure medicine and his erection withered. She suggested I eat lots of celery instead.

Over Christmas and New Year's, Annie flew to Mississippi to visit her mother and her sister, who had just flown in from England. Annie told her sister that things didn't look too good for us. Her practical sister said, "You're forty years old. Where are you going to go?"

Annie didn't know.

Margot and I spent New Year's Eve at my house, both of us heaving from the twenty-four-hour flu. We cleaned the house and Margot cooked for me. Fried chicken. We couldn't eat it.

We fed the flesh to Sophie and went to bed with fevers.

On New Year's Day, Margot was determined to beat the flu with a six-mile march along the beach. "I will not surrender to this," she said, stopping to throw up every mile or so.

Maybe it was the flu that started it. She turned on me: "Why do you think you deserve two women in your life? Who do you think you are?"

Later, I remembered that this was a question my mother asked me whenever I delivered precocious teenage opinions about God's existence or nonexistence. "Who do you think you are, Bill?" Mom asked.

"Margot, don't forget about the war being over," I reminded her.

"But this isn't fun anymore. It has to be more fun than not-fun."

She said she was thinking of leaving her photo shop job and moving to this side of Long Island Sound, maybe working in the Wading River post office.

She also informed me that I had given her a sex disease. Venereal warts. Dozens of little lumps. They had been burned off and it wasn't fun having warts burned off.

I apologized.

"I think you forgot your tart-in-training manual," I tried, embarrassed about the warts.

But she wasn't laughing. We marched back to the house, heaving along the way.

"All I want is equal time with Annie," Margot said on the drive back to the Orient Point ferry. She bought a copy of the local paper and scanned the real estate section.

I said I'd help her hunt for a place the next time she came over.

"You mean the next time Annie visits her mother," Margot snapped and ran onto the ferry.

I coughed my way to the bar and tried to bring down my fever with double Wild Turkeys. "She's serious, that one," said Sean, the bartender, after I confessed my Margot quandary with him. "In fact, it sounds to me like she's got the picket fence and the cottage all picked out for you."

My heart had started a peculiar pinging pain. To quiet the pinging, I rode my bike all week wildly through the woods. Exhaustion calmed my heart.

In the woods, I longed for a bush to flare into flame. It would have been so easy, just a little bush on fire. A sign that somebody was in control of all this.

The doctor said I had developed an extra heartbeat. A palpitation. If it didn't stop soon he would prescribe heart tranquilizers. He reminded me about my blood pressure and the medicine I should be taking for that. "This is serious," he said.

When I mentioned celery, he said, "Don't be ridiculous."

At the bar, hacking and palpitating, I told Sean: "Why don't I just forget it with Margot? She's twenty-five, could have lots of kids. But what do I want with kids? I'd rather spend a winter with Annie and save my heart. We're happy enough in our paradise for two."

"At least you know her. Margot's the unknown."

"I think Margot's a leaver. She left her last boyfriend."

Sean poured me one on the house. "You ought to do something about that cough."

Our baby was conceived in the snow in a pine woods. A few towns away from where Annie pouted in her motel room and fashioned the final draft of *Seductions*.

We couldn't bed down in the house, because Annie might drive up at any moment. Recently she had delivered a new black-and-white TV set to replace the one she took with her. The TV was her gift because she felt bad about "the way she had treated me."

I skulked around town with Margot, wearing dark glasses. We looked at property advertised in the classifieds, cheap dumps like mine.

As we lay in the snow in the pine woods, Margot put it bluntly: "I have fallen in love with you."

I pulled up my pants, zippered my coat, brushed off the snow, and stared at the winter sky. "I am a dead man," I said.

She left on the ferry, ashen and sobbing, her black hair dripping melting snow.

At the bar I was hit with a startling idea. "Why can't I live with both of them?" I asked Sean.

"You want to know why? They would crucify you, that's why. I tried it once. Each one takes a hand and they nail you to a tree."

That's what I knew about Margot so far.

At the New London Golden Panda I needed more details of her life.

We ordered dessert and a liqueur. "We're getting married," Margot told the waiter.

He served us complimentary Benedictine.

We skipped out of the place and up the hill and the three flights to her apartment.

Inside of Margot, our child was now about the size of a spring peeper tadpole.

About two o'clock, Margot woke me from my blissful stupor. "There's blood here," she said, switching on the lamp by her mattress and studying her blood-smudged fingers.

There was blood on the sheet, too. A small spot.

She went into the bathroom, put in a tampon. She turned off the light and we fell back into our bliss.

Just before dawn, I woke in an immense stickiness. I fumbled for the light. The mattress, Margot's nightgown, and my T-shirt were blood-soaked.

I woke her and we stared at the blood, sobering up, gradually realizing what was happening to us, what we were losing.

I gathered some towels and a box of Kotex from the bathroom. We threw the sheets into the corner, followed by the towels and Kotex as we used them up.

I was about to telephone for an ambulance when Margot noticed that the flow seemed to be slowing, that perhaps she would not bleed to death.

We watched the sky lighten over the Thames River, baffled that our hope had been killed so quickly. We didn't even have a chance to try out a name for our child.

At sunrise, I showered the blood off, washing minuscule bits of our child down the shower-stall drain.

In the New London morning, I searched for an open drug-store with Super Kotex. I returned an hour later with several boxes. But Margot didn't need them.

The crisis was over.

Only the medical details remained.

Margot called her doctor and he met her at the hospital.

"Does this mean I can't have any more babies?" Margot asked. He assured her that she could have dozens of children. She just needed a D and C.

While we waited at reception for a room assignment, her doctor's office called the head nurse with the results of her pregnancy test.

"Negative," the nurse informed us.

"But yesterday they told her it was positive!" I hollered.

"That's not what they say today," the nurse scowled.

She pushed the papers toward us to sign.

I scribbled my signature and identified my relationship. "I am/am not the father of this child/this not-child."

For a few hours we sat in a semiprivate room, waiting, while the sun slanted through the blinds. We had nothing to say to each other, couldn't speak. There wouldn't even be a funeral for our maybe baby.

Just before dark, the surgeon and the anesthetist arrived. They told us what was to be done: a general anesthesia, a scraping of Margot's insides. About forty minutes from start to finish.

After the operation, the surgeon visited me in the waiting room. "She's fine," he said. "She'll be rocky for a bit, but tomorrow if all goes well she can go home."

"Was she pregnant?"

"Oh, yes. Our office was in error. I found bits of necrological tissue in the discharge."

"Bits of the child."

"Of the fetus."

He shook my hand and walked away.

I sat with Margot until midnight, but she was too groggy and depressed to care.

That night I slept in her apartment on the mattress stained with dried blood with a clean sheet over it. Across the Thames River at the Groton submarine base, the machines buzzed and whistles shrilled—the night shift constructing a new nuclear sub. They were on a seven-day, twenty-four-hour schedule. It was 1983. The arms race was at a furor.

In the morning I brought Margot back from the hospital.

From a phone booth, I called Annie at her motel and explained something about a sick friend and I probably wouldn't be back in my house for a few days.

Annie told me how she had spent that night: "There was a

huge thunderstorm here. In March, a thunderstorm! I didn't know where you were. And it poured with rain. I was on my knees, praying in the thunder and the lightning, 'Please, please, please!' I didn't know who I was praying to. I just prayed for hours. 'Please, oh please!'"

9

White Wine

I SAT ALONE at Sean's Pub on Sunday afternoon of Memorial Day weekend. I shouldn't have ordered the wine. I had a date to meet Annie at a barge party in a few minutes and I didn't want to show up befuddled.

But it was a pretty afternoon. All Sean's patrons were at the beach. I needed his private counseling.

I ordered a second glass of wine.

"Tell me, Sean, where is it written that a man can't have two women?"

Sean ignored me and cleaned the bar, bored with my constant questioning.

"You've got to make up your mind, Bill. Stop being so damn passive."

"How can I hurt either one of them? I love them both."

Late for the barge party, I chugged the second glass of wine into an empty stomach and rushed out into the hot afternoon sun.

A few steps from the pub was an empty phone booth. Spurred by my wine infusion, I dialed Margot's number at her parents' place. Why? I'd wish her a happy Memorial Day. That's it. That was an excuse.

Margot answered.

"I'm coming to visit in a few days. Which one is good for you?" I asked.

"None of them. I can't see you."

"Why?"

"I decided it's over. All the other girls are with their boyfriends this weekend. I'm alone. I can't do this any more."

"Come on, Margot. Where's your sense of humor?"

"It's not funny now. I've been crying for days."

"But remember, the war's over if you . . ."

"You can't come here. You're not very popular with my dad now and he's right by this phone."

Dad, the security chief and Korean Army vet, who carried a pistol.

"Margot . . ."

"No, I won't see you again. You won't even give me equal time with Annie. I carried your baby, I had a D and C, and still you won't give me equal time. All that night I lay in that hospital bed wondering how I'd messed up my life by getting involved with you. You know what I really wanted? You gone, and my old boyfriend back. I dreamed of him then, not you."

"But I was overjoyed about the kid! Remember the champagne? How happy I was for us?"

"I remember warts. I remember Annie moving out of your house and you not inviting me to move in. That's what I remember! And you want me to laugh!"

"I do! I do! Laugh!"

"No way."

"What day?"

"Don't call again."

She hung up.

I was a man released from limbo. The young mother of my only for-sure child had just betrayed me.

I fled to my car and drove east along the coast of the sound.

At the barge party, Annie waved to me from across the deck. The May sun had tanned her and bleached her hair. Her smile shone against the tan. She had finished her novel at the motel and bought a house nearby, all on her own with a loan from Lady Beatrice. Things were looking up for her.

I waved back and headed for the bar before joining her. An older woman stood at the bar, a stranger.

"I'm upset," I greeted the stranger.

"That's too bad," she said.

"Let me ask you a question. OK?"

"Sure."

"Why can't a man have more than one woman at the same time?"

"Why not? Seems all right to me."

"Exactly."

Having established my rights, I headed out across the barge and tried my question on more women. All agreed with the drinking man that there was no rule that said he couldn't have two girlfriends at once.

Annie, noticing my fuzzy condition, suggested I needed some dinner. She would cook it at her new house.

She guided me to the exit, and drove me off.

Annie's house was a three-bedroom, two-story job with a deck overlooking the sound and two bathrooms and two washing machines: one for clothes, one for dishes.

Annie gave me the tour.

The house was mostly empty of furniture, but on the second floor, at the door to the deck, was a baby's crib, left by the previous owners.

"We'll never need that," I said, pointing to the crib. "Funny they should leave it."

Annie said the child had been born brain-damaged and lived in a shelter for the retarded now.

We sat on the bare deck and I sipped another glass of wine, determined to obliterate myself and forget Margot. I'd concentrate on her horrendous piano playing.

"Annie, it's just you and me from now on. You're the only loyal person I know. I don't care if we can't have a child. I trust you. You searched for me in a city of eight million. I want to be with you no matter what. You are the real McCoy." I babbled, choking up.

She regarded me. "Why are you saying this?"

"That time I said I was away in New York, I was with a girl named Margot in New London. She was pregnant. She lost the kid as soon as she got the news the test was positive. Almost as if she had to lose it. But it's all over now. And I haven't got any more secrets."

Annie sipped her wine and studied her new view across the sound. "It sounds like Margot and you are pretty serious."

"Not anymore," I blurted, suddenly terrified that Annie would split too.

"You and Margot should probably go away for a few months and figure it out between you."

"No!"

We sat silently.

"I still don't know what to say. I'm no housewife. I have dreams for myself. The idea of a kid still makes me nervous. The alcoholism on both sides. All of it."

"I told you. I just need you. We probably won't have a child. It doesn't matter. *You* matter, Annie. You and I matter. That's all."

I put my arm around her. We kissed.

"Stop," she said, wiping away my tears. "Stop."

"You know what convinced me it was only you for me?"

"What?"

"The TV set you brought. Even though you moved out you still cared. You didn't want me to be alone, so you brought the TV."

"Oh."

The next morning I woke in Annie's house alone.

Attached to the crib was a note that she had gone to town and would be right back.

She returned with a pornographic library: *Penthouse, Playboy, Club, Swank,* and an X-rated video review. "I bought these at the drugstore. I was so embarrassed," she said. "They looked at me like I was trash."

She tossed the magazines on the bed. "You study these. I'll be right back. We are going to fuck like bunnies for seven days, even if it hurts. My time is now. It's perfect. I'll go roll a joint. That Margot woman is not going to have our baby."

We fucked like bunnies.

After each session, Annie lay with her head back over the side of the bed and her feet high up the wall, so that not a single sperm escaped the meeting with her single aging ovary.

"Sean says every other day is best, to conserve sperm," I mentioned, aching and tired, on day three.

"And I say bunnies know best," Annie said.

On the seventh day, Annie too was beat. We'd done our best, I suggested. We were past her ovulation peak.

"Nope," Annie concluded. "There's probably one last egg in there. The very last one. And today's the day."

She yanked off my pants. "That girl will not have our baby."

Afterward, Annie threw her legs up against the wall. "That was the one!" she proclaimed, upside down.

The next day she was even more certain.

"It's happened! I know it has! I feel like a balloon that's just filled up. I'm *special!*"

— 10

Sophie's Beach

I EXPECTED NOTHING.

This was probably just another Annie drama. I'd wait for the test, which would probably be negative. If I didn't hope, I couldn't be hurt.

The idea of a child was still just that. An idea.

I would stay as still as a stone, in Annie's house.

In early July, Frank Stiffel invited us to his home.

Frank had survived Treblinka, the Warsaw ghetto, and Auschwitz, and had written a memoir that had been rejected by publishers for forty years. The market was satiated with survivors' accounts, the publishers calculated. I had just offered to publish Frank's memoir in my overlooked manuscript series, following Paul Rogers's novel. I called the series the Editors' Book Award. To be eligible, a manuscript had to be rejected by everybody everywhere.

I was in awe of Frank. At the death camps, and in his life since then, Frank practiced the kind of gentleness that preachers only preached about.

On the way to Flushing, Annie and I detoured to Stony Brook

Hospital for a pregnancy blood test. A brief stop, we thought. Draw some blood. Leave.

Annie checked in and sat down as directed, a middle-aged woman in a hospital lobby.

The nurse went out to lunch for forty-five minutes. "Are you still here?" she asked, when she got back.

The test was done, and Annie and I returned to the car. "They didn't care much about me. No big news to them, I guess," she said.

We hurried down the Long Island Expressway. I was anxious for Frank and his wife, Ione, to meet Annie.

Being ignored at the hospital reminded Annie of Margot. "How could you have done that to me? I mean, you hurt me so badly. How could you just have gone and done that?" She was losing control, her face a puffy mass.

I considered pulling over, calling Frank, and canceling our dinner.

I tried to justify my passion with Margot. I reminded Annie of our confusion. But to Annie it all amounted to a vast offense against her. She cried until she was exhausted.

We drove on toward Queens.

Rather than continue in silence, I handed her Frank's manuscript, *The Tale of the Ring: A Kaddish,* and asked her to read it if she felt like it. "Out loud," I suggested. Now and then she did.

Annie read of Frank as a Jewish teenager in Poland, planning to be a great poet and a doctor. In 1939, the Russians invaded his town of Lvov and then the Germans after them. Frank's mother and father and most of his family were wiped out. Only a few tattered and creased photographs remained to illustrate his memoir.

Frank was sent to Treblinka by boxcar for execution. He escaped and wandered the Polish countryside, pretending to be a Catholic, praising Christ to one and all. He was exposed and denounced as an imposter and imprisoned in Auschwitz. There he survived because of the miracle of the Girl in the Ring, a ring he found in the mud with the image of Ione on it. He would not meet Ione until after the war, and did not know it was she.

Annie read the key passage. Frank finds the ring in the filth of Treblinka. "And there, watching me intently, as if she were trying to call me back to my senses, was the Girl. I bent down and picked up the ring. It was a heavy piece of gold set around a chunk of tiger's eye stone with a soft cameo of a girl's face carved into it. Perhaps I had become an easy prey to superstition by now, but as I clutched the Ring, I had a vivid sensation of holding the Spirit of Life."

Because he believed that he would one day meet the Girl, he survived and helped others to live. He hated no one, then or now, not even his captors.

After liberation, he met the Girl, Ione, on top of a truckload of chestnuts while wandering in the Apennine Mountains of Italy.

Annie read: "I was frozen and half-asleep. While my companions were trying to make conversation with the girl, I fell into a deep slumber. I dreamed of Mother and the way I had seen her the last time, on the train to Treblinka. She caressed my cheek. I felt something soft and warm around my throat, and a melodious, familiar voice said, 'Take it. You are cold.'

"And I knew. I knew for certain. I opened my eyes. I was wide awake. The exquisite oval of the beautiful face was above me. She was smiling with warmth.

"It was the Girl of the Ring."

Ione and Frank were married in Rome a few months later.

"This is a real love story I wish I could live," Annie said.

Frank and the Girl in the Ring greeted us at the door to their row house. Auschwitz camp number 107455 was tattooed on his arm.

Annie and I sat with them in the small backyard under their one tree.

We did not talk about the book, or the war.

Ione cooked more Italian food than we could eat and Frank poured more wine than we could drink. Later, their daughter, Aurora, joined us.

I felt hugely blessed to be Frank's publisher, to be with his family. Ione was not only an image on a ring, she was kind and beautiful and young in every way. How had Frank known he would find her? What directed him to that road to Rome and a wagon full of chestnuts?

What was the spirit behind all this feasting, this joy?

I looked at Frank, this mild, slight man, at his eyes that had seen total degradation and prevailed.

I was overwhelmed by his strength, out of my depth in mystery.

In his memoir and in his life, Frank was teaching me the defiant strength of love.

Back home in Wading River, at Annie's house—now our house—we waited for news of the pregnancy test.

Dr. Livoti's office called Stony Brook Hospital for the results. The hospital said the lab was backed up.

For several days, the hospital said, "Not ready yet."

A week later, Annie asked Livoti's assistant if she had remembered to call the hospital. She hadn't. She would.

Days later, they still had no word. They were terribly busy, the assistant explained. In fact, at that moment Dr. Livoti was on an emergency cesarean.

For sure, they would telephone us tomorrow.

We sat near the phone the next day from eight to five.

At five, Annie called Livoti's office again. It was closing time, but a voice answered. When Annie complained, the voice said, "I'm only a temp."

"We've been waiting for two whole weeks! I have to know if I have a baby in me!" Annie cried.

"I think I saw a memo around here," the temp said. "We'll call tomorrow. I have to go home now."

"For the sake of all humanity," Annie pleaded, "if you have any sense of decency, look for that memo now!"

The temp said she'd try. She hung up.

"She won't ever call," Annie said. "It's nothing to them. Hundreds of tests a week. What can a temporary secretary care? Am I supposed to get down on my knees? Please let that phone ring."

Instantly it rang.

"Mrs. McCoy?" It was the harassed temp.

"Yes?"

"The result is positive."

"Positive!" Annie shouted, and leaped up.

"Positive!" I cheered.

I kissed her cheek and held her and steadied her shaking hand. Together we hung up the phone.

It was July 19, 1983.

This might actually be happening, I thought. Annie had known the truth. She *was* special.

Sophie, whose spaying had started it all, pranced into the room, begging a walk.

"We'll celebrate at Sophie's Beach!" Annie said.

Sophie's Beach was a long mud bank on a marshy inlet. Now and then local fishermen launched their boats there, and in the nights parked lovers used the dirt road leading up to it. But on this cool, gray evening with a drizzle falling, the three of us had it alone.

I brought along Sophie's supply of used tennis balls and a bottle of champagne. We set up a bar on the hood of the Chevy and toasted the universe, while Sophie jumped off the mud banks into the bay with gigantic splashes and paddled off to retrieve thrown balls. Sophie, our child after Rocky and Ellen, our dead ersatz children.

The champagne was Annie's farewell to booze. She knocked it back, stripped down, and plunged into the inlet, naked.

"How do you feel?" I called through the drizzle.

"Incredibly high!"

Sophie splashed after more balls while Annie swam far out into the mist, her face up to the rain. I sat on the car hood and sipped.

Much later, soaking dog, towel-draped Annie, and I left Sophie's Beach in the twilight and headed toward her new house.

Everything was about to change for us. Slowly I was beginning to hope that.

_11_

Being Pregnant

ON THE DAY before her forty-first birthday, Annie took a bus to New York for her first checkup. Carol Livoti hurried to the door. "We did it! We did it!" she said, hugging and kissing Annie. "So quickly! What did we do right?"

The nurse prepared Annie for her examination. "Congratulations, Mrs. McCoy," she said.

Then Dr. Livoti listened through her stethoscope for the new child's heartbeat.

"Here. You listen," she said, handing the tip to Annie and plugging the earpieces into her ears.

Annie heard the determined heartbeat, faint but definite, of her two-and-a-half-month-old child. She listened and cried while the doctor held her hand.

"It's a special baby," said Carol. "One ovary, at your age, very rare. Now we just have to make sure it stays in there."

She explained to Annie about her occasional blood "spotting" that usually did not signal a miscarriage and was nothing to be anxious about.

The first three months were the most worrisome. Annie should avoid sex, exercise mildly, and not worry about spotting.

Back home, Annie was the amazement of her friends. . . . "Knocked up at forty-one! Jeez, the scandal!" laughed Barbara Springs, the seventy-four-year-old keeper of local records. Barbara's own birth had been premature. At seven months she had been left in a shoebox to die, so she swore. "They didn't think I had a chance, so they wrapped me up and put me away in the shoebox until I'd stop breathing. I fooled them!"

At parties, Annie told stories, cracked jokes, and shone gloriously. Because she was ecstatic, others were, too. Every other event—someone's new book, someone else's next divorce—was nothing. Her conception of a child, against the odds, was a local wonder.

One morning, lying in bed, she felt a flutter in her womb and was astounded at the life in her. Bending over to slip a shoe on, she was slightly obstructed by her growing middle, and marveled at the growth.

Gradually she began to show her pregnancy. Strangers stepped aside in line at the A&P to let her pass. People held doors open for her. Women she had never met touched her belly in appreciation. "If only people would always treat each other like this," Annie said.

For once she knew a certainty. Gone were her drunk parents, loving one day, lost in booze the next; forgotten, the string of one-night stands, the disappearance of friends into marriage or death.

"I know it's a cliché, but I feel like I'm the only woman in the world who ever had a baby," she exulted.

She tried out names for "it"—Davis Debutts, an old Virginia family name, if a boy; Holly Springs if a girl.

I crossed off the days until the child was at less risk for miscarriage, each day more and more convinced that this child might actually make it.

The news around us was not good: fear of nuclear holocaust had neared a universal panic. With most of the country, Annie and I watched an ABC TV movie, *The Day After*, about the atomic end in Lawrence, Kansas. That just couldn't happen to us or our child.

NBC's "Today" show invited callers to talk with chief disarmament advisor Kenneth Adelman. When a young girl asked him, "What if nuclear war starts by accident?" he had no answer for her.

In Maine, an eleven-year-old girl, Samantha Smith, wrote Soviet chief Brezhnev, pleading for disarmament. He invited her to Moscow to plead in person. When Samantha was killed in a plane crash, she was declared a national martyr.

"Nuclear War Can Ruin Your Entire Day" was a popular Wading River bumper sticker. The local paper featured a cartoon, showing President Reagan holding a lit match in a sea of gasoline. Title: "Nuclear proliferation." Periodically the *New York Times* showed the nuclear Doomsday clock of the Union of Concerned Scientists. It was seconds to midnight and counting down.

Out in the sound, the nuclear subs prowled. We were twenty-five miles from the submarine headquarters of the country. Ground Zero.

Carl MacIntire, my father's favorite evangelist and still on the radio, welcomed the End because that's when Jesus would judge the sinners and take Christians to heaven with Him. "Any day now," MacIntire promised. "Any day."

I offered to publish an anthology of PEN writers and donate the income to the Union of Concerned Scientists. I told *The New Yorker*'s Jonathan Schell that I would print one million paperbacks of his nuclear warning, *The Fate of the Earth*, and give them away. Somehow, I told him, I would find the money to do that. But neither project worked out.

Dutifully, I mailed small contributions to Physicians for Social Responsibility.

While the child in Annie added cell to cell, I worried too about becoming a father like my pop, a daily drudge. I found little to say in my journal beyond the surmise about nuclear winter and the suburbanization of my spirit.

One day I decided to kill off Bill Henderson. I'd re-create myself as a pseudonymous eighteen-year-old author, a wild kid, unencumbered by reputation or chores, with nothing to lose, who would write anything as long as it was the blunt truth. As my child approached, I would become a child again myself—if only at the typewriter.

One bright day, in a note thumbtacked to the wall, I proclaimed the birth of this new writing kid, Willie Charles.

But Willie Charles was stillborn. He never uttered a yawp. His father had more important things to do . . . paying bills, publishing books, answering the mail, worrying about the End.

I tried another cure for suburban bomb angst. From now on I would create for God alone. Nothing I wrote would be for publication. In that way I would be free to think and write anything, sending it all up to God unencumbered.

But God was an unresponsive reader.

Annie was affected by none of these moods. Every day was bliss to her, and she suffered not a twinge of morning sickness. Annie was in direct contact with the world's foundation. She was the youth I dreamed about creating with Willie Charles.

But the spotting continued, and many mornings by more than just a drop or two, a constant nagging omen.

On August 3, with Carol Livoti's OK, Annie decided to fly to Mississippi to visit her mother, who had suddenly sobered up.

In the women's bathroom of LaGuardia Airport, just before takeoff, Annie discovered a mass of blood in her pants. Padding herself with wads of paper towels, she made it to a phone and hysterically called Dr. Livoti.

"Be calm, find a place to lie down," Carol said, as if she was not surprised that this was happening at Annie's age, and Annie should not be so shocked either.

Annie lay down on the stone floor while passengers scurried around her, paying no attention. She knew the baby was going or gone. She lay there and heard the loudspeaker proclaiming landings, departures, and warnings about terrorists. She listened to the scream of jets taking off and braking, an anonymous woman on the floor, stifling her own screams.

An hour later the bleeding had not increased. In the bathroom, she replaced the paper towels in her pants. She hobbled to a taxi.

In Manhattan, she collapsed on the couch of a friend and tried not to move for twenty-four hours.

The bleeding stopped.

She took off for Mississippi after calling me. "I had a little scare. It's OK now."

After three months, Annie and I thought the baby would stay where it was. We could risk an Annie-cooked, candlelit, seafood pasta dinner, a half-glass of wine for Annie.

And sex.

On Sunday morning, still vigorous with the previous night's passion, I drove to the village for fresh bagels and the Sunday *Times*. It was a cool, bright September morning.

In the kitchen, Annie cooked her special Holly Springs breakfast—eggs, ham, and grits with red-eye gravy. She sang to the Gershwin on the record player.

Slowly, down the inside of her thigh, she felt a trickle, then a drip. At her feet, a bloody clot formed.

Annie ran for the bathroom, her bare feet leaving bloody tracks behind her. The drip became a gush. She threw up her nightgown and thrust her hands into her crotch to stop the flow. When she removed her hands she held chunks of something. Because she couldn't stop the flow, she began to sort through it, looking for her baby.

Back from the store, I found Annie in the bathroom, smeared with blood, still frantically examining what was flooding out.

We said nothing.

I helped her into a reclining chair, the same chair in which my mother had lain dying. "Just stay here. I'll call Carol," I said. But at that hour, I reached only her answering machine.

Annie lay back in the recliner, crying softly, sopping up the blood with the towels I brought.

"We have to get to New York," I said, and rushed off in the car to find an open gas station. The tank was nearly empty.

At the station, I hammered the steering wheel with my fist while the sleepy gas-pumping attendant regarded me warily. "Live! Live! Live!" I shouted.

I struggled to reach the child inside Annie. I saw it in an epic struggle to survive, gasping, clawing, hanging on against rapids of blood. I was the child's cheerleader, reaching out for its mind, soul, and spirit, fusing my will with its will, my strength with its strength. "Hang in there kid," I bellowed.

Speeding back to Annie, I prayed to Mom wherever she was. "Please help us, Mom. Please!" I needed her and all the power she could find. I needed Mom's God.

Why had I bothered Annie with sex the night before? If I had quelled my lust, my child would be alive now.

At home, Annie lay in Mom's old chair and prayed: "We didn't have much in common, Mrs. Henderson. But can you help me now? Please stop the bleeding?" Annie looked into the rising sun.

When I hurried in, Annie was on the phone with Dr. Livoti. "Big gobs of stuff fell out, my whole insides," Annie said. "I think my baby came out."

"Keep your feet up and see me when the bleeding stops," Livoti said. For now, Annie was to rest and not attempt the trip into the city.

Annie lay all day in the recliner. The bleeding slowed but did not stop. She drifted off into bad dreams.

Two days later the bleeding did stop. "I think your mom answered my prayers," Annie said.

I doubted it.

We set out for New York. As instructed by Livoti, Annie lay cushioned in the back of the old Chevy on a lawn chair mattress. We were scheduled for a sonogram examination, a new procedure.

It rained. I waited in commuter jams at mid-Island and again in Queens, wondering how Annie could hold back despair. I knew her womb was an empty place. There was nothing to see there with the new sonogram gadget.

We stopped. We started and stopped again. Just before noon we parked on East Sixty-eighth Street outside of the laboratory that Dr. Livoti had directed us to.

"Hello, Mrs. McCoy, and you must be Mr. McCoy," a peppy nurse said. She led Annie to the changing room.

I was told to be seated next to a stack of family magazines featuring happy moms and pops and kids. I wondered if I would throw up. This was just a wake, a technical wake, for a child that had vanished.

Now they were gazing at an empty place in Annie. Soon they would arrive and tell me the unfortunate news.

I was crippled with sorrow. Again, as with Margot's baby, there wouldn't even be a funeral.

The nurse peeked around the corner of a partition. "Mr. McCoy." She grinned. "Would you like to see your child?"

I had no idea what she was talking about. I stared at her.

"Would you like to see your child? Come with me." She motioned. I followed.

In a small room, Annie lay on a table with her belly exposed. Over her was a sort of grainy TV screen. Annie was smiling at me.

"Just watch the screen, Mr. McCoy," said the doctor after shaking my hand. He passed an instrument over Annie's middle and pointed out the features of her womb. He mentioned something about a polyp, a bruise, and then, "over here, out of harm's way, here's your baby." He pointed his finger at a tiny body with a head, two legs, and arms. Arms waving at us. The child was waving! Hello, hello!

"Hello to you too," I gulped, and then I waved back.

My knees shuddered. I collapsed on a stool, wordless at the first sight of our resurrected child.

Later, Dr. Livoti mailed us the sonogram negatives: two sheets of eighteen black-and-white three-by-two-inch images. Our child lies in shadows on what seems like a moonlit beach, cushioned in sand dunes.

Dr. Livoti said the sonogram was a modern marvel. A few years before this, after so much bleeding, the child might have been scraped out at a local hospital in a routine D and C operation.

Carol called it "my sonogram baby."

~12

Marriage

AFTER PARTYING with Caruso, Annie's grandfather staggered back to the Virginia mansion some nights, drunk and singing. Then his daughter, Frances, nursed him the next morning so that he could make it to his office at the Southern Railroad.

Frances liked nursing. In 1932, she studied it at Montreal's McGill University, planning to help people as she helped her dad. After graduation, longing for something idealistic, she joined FDR's TVA project as a nurse at the Chickamauga Dam construction site.

There she met H. Davis McCoy, from Mississippi, the young head doctor at the infirmary. They married. Soon a baby was due. To pay his family's bills and to avoid the everyday boring complaints of workers at the dam, Dr. McCoy became a specialist, a pathologist. He also composed verses about the bugs he examined under his microscope. A poet of the sub-world.

They moved to Montreal where a baby girl, Annie's sister Beatrice, was born. For two years they were happy and Frances was a teetotaler, as she had always been.

The war changed that.

Just before Annie was born, Dr. McCoy showed up in uniform and announced he had signed with the Army Medical Corps. The war would be his grand adventure, his grail quest. In the fall of 1942, he left for Europe and spent the next three years tending to casualties. On D-Day, he followed the first wave of soldiers ashore. At war's end, he tried too late to sign up for duty in the Pacific.

He returned to his wife and two daughters, restless, bored, and drinking. For a while he taught pathology in Seattle, then at the Oxnard Clinic in New Orleans. They lived in an old barracks under the Huey P. Long bridge—mildew and lizards everywhere.

When New Orleans society refused to recognize her elder daughter's coming-out, or to even notice that Frances existed in her barracks under the bridge, she began to drink in the evenings with her husband. Drinking became what they did together.

Dr. McCoy was asked to leave the clinic.

He found another job in Holly Springs, Mississippi, as head pathologist for a new hospital.

In their Holly Springs apartment, his wife gave up. Her growing daughters didn't need her any more. She was not permitted to work. She woke with a drink and spent the day with a drink.

At Christmas and Thanksgiving, Frances honored the old Virginia ceremonies. She cooked the dinner with the maid's help. She hung the decorations and set the table with her family's best china and silverware. But she seldom made it to dinner. Annie and Beatrice often found her in the dry bathtub, dressed in her nightgown, unable to rise.

The sisters served the dinner to themselves and waited for Dr. McCoy to return from wherever he was.

The next year, Dr. McCoy moved his family into a proper Holly Springs house. Summer nights he would sit on the front steps of his proper house in his underwear, drinking and reciting his bug poems to the sleeping neighborhood.

In the 1950s Alcoholics Anonymous was not a chic social club. Booze was a family secret that made the McCoys special. Annie lived in her room, with her Cokes and her junk food and her Nancy Drew books and her secrets. Most evenings she and her sister ventured downstairs only when their parents had passed out. Together, they kept order in their world.

After the girls left home for boarding school and college, Dr. McCoy and his wife went on benders together. Two- and three-day benders. Once, the frantic maid called Annie in New York and Annie flew to Holly Springs, where she found her parents under their bed. She telephoned for an ambulance and watched them carried away on stretchers.

Dr. McCoy's colleagues at the hospital hushed it up.

Years later, after his boozy misdiagnosis possibly caused a patient's death, Dr. McCoy repented and sobered up for good. But for Frances there was nothing else to do. She was a Virginia lady in a lesser land.

When he retired, Dr. McCoy was forced to spend the days with his wife but there was no way to cure her. She was long lost from her daddy's mansion. For what had happened to her, Dr. McCoy took the blame.

At seventy-two, he fled from her to a Tennessee diet clinic, declaring he would lose twenty-eight pounds in a month. But it was his life he wanted to lose when he died in Annie's arms that March 11, 1982.

After the funeral, Frances commented, "We ended badly."

She destroyed his papers and letters, and flushed him from her life.

Now she lived alone in an apartment, Heaven Hill free again on doctor's orders. Most of her friends had died. Her only companion was Druscilla, the black family maid, who had protected her through all of it.

"But you are too old to have a child," her mother mentioned quietly, when we proudly told her of Annie's pregnancy. "And besides, you aren't married."

Then she began telephoning every near and distant relative throughout the South. Annie had been seduced by this Northern cad! Not married!

To Frances, this pregnancy was the worst rape of the South

and her family name since the Civil War. The second cousins telephoned the third cousins and soon the angry calls and letters had reduced Annie to anxious exhaustion.

If sex hadn't caused a miscarriage, Annie's mother might. To save our baby, we had to get married, fast.

I worried that the needle of the premarital blood test might bring on a miscarriage. It didn't.

But more than the needle, and her mother's assault, the very idea of marriage was enough to make Annie miscarry. Annie knew of only one marriage up close. Her parents'. To Annie, marriage was death.

Annie still considered herself a great actress in hiding. In marriage there would be no reviews or curtain calls. And what about Prince Charming? Wasn't he supposed to show up some day? Was this all there was? Chained to a little publisher, a borderline welfare case? Like her mother, swept away to a barracks under a bridge, she was forsaking the good life forever.

To ease her panic, I told Annie that a marriage was just a convenience, a practical matter done for others. Like taking out a dog license.

Somehow the dog license metaphor didn't work for Annie. This had to be more than that.

I also knew that if we didn't quiet her mother, I would let the old woman have it about her attempts to kill our child.

And so we were married on September 29, 1983.

I worked in my garage until the last minute and then I couldn't find a tie. Could one be married without a tie? As we rushed down the road toward the town hall, we stopped at a friend's house and borrowed a red tie with a large brown splotch of something on it.

Annie wore a blue ballooning dress to cover her belly and in her hair a fancy fake rose she had picked up the day before at a yard sale.

"I'm feeling strange," she said, as we pulled into the parking lot.

I asked the justice of the peace to make it quick, since my fiancée was not feeling well. With his secretary as a witness, we started the ceremony in his office.

"I feel faint," Annie said, sitting down.

"There's a nice cherry tree in the front yard and fresh air, too," the secretary said.

I helped Annie to her feet and we hurried outside.

"We can stop this here," I said. "Marriage isn't worth a miscarriage."

Annie shook her head.

As I clutched her arm so that she wouldn't topple over, the kind.justice sped through his words and our responses.

Then, from the town hall pay phone, Annie called her mother off.

$\sim$13

Love Is God

IN 1983, "amnio" was what every pregnant woman over thirty-five was expected to endure. At Annie's age, the fetus was 10 percent more likely to have Down's Syndrome or to suffer other deformities like spina bifida. Through a long needle plunged into Annie's abdomen, Dr. Livoti would withdraw fluid and check it for genetic abnormalities.

Amniocentesis was not a therapeutic test. If the fetus was deformed, it could not be fixed. Abortion was advised. All of this had to be done before the end of the second trimester, the legal limit for abortions.

But we had seen our child waving at us. Annie had felt it moving about in her and she had listened to its heartbeat. To us, this was a person right now, and to have it declared deformed and unworthy of life was unthinkable. In short, murder.

Besides, what exactly was the definition of deformed? Two heads? No head? Three arms? Half a nose? What made the child too much of an inconvenience to permit it to live, I wondered.

Doctors and politicians played with definitions of *deformity* and *life* much as medieval theologians toyed with inventorying angels on pinheads. But the real "lifestyle" argument was convenience—deformed children were an inconvenience. The style of the times.

But we had been assured, and assured ourselves, that the amniocentesis test was wise. We could decide after the test results about what to do.

Dr. Livoti warned us of a 2-percent chance that the act of inserting the needle alone would produce a spontaneous abortion. And to that I added the risks of bouncing along the hellish Long Island Expressway to New York.

On October 2 we rode the bus to the city, sitting in the middle to cushion shocks. We stayed with friends and woke the next morning to bounce across town on the Ninety-sixth Street bus to the doctor's East Side office, the same office where the child had waved to us weeks earlier. Annie was required to fill her bladder for the test, and each bounce hurt.

Again we were greeted with, "Good morning, Mr. McCoy and Mrs. McCoy," and Annie was led away for the test, which they promised would not hurt a bit despite the huge needle and the lack of anesthesia.

In the next room, Annie watched as the needle was prepared, but felt only a dull numbness as it was inserted, shielded from her sight, deep into her womb.

Outside in the waiting room, I again prepared for an agonizing announcement and was again summoned by the same nurse with, "Mr. McCoy, would you like to see your baby?" Annie lay on the same table under the same sonogram screen.

The child did not wave this time. It seemed to be sleeping.

We were told to wait until November 10. On that date we would know if an abortion was suggested. The 10-percent chance.

I prepared to be patient. But I have trouble waiting five minutes for a restaurant table. They were asking for five weeks, for my entire life.

Through the rest of October, the child grew quietly in Annie. On October 19, she visited the doctor again and listened to her baby's determined heartbeat.

At home, she and Paula continued to hoot and revise their novel.

In my garage office, I watched the leaves fall, the sun lower toward the horizon, the wind turn cold, and the year ending. The year 1984, Orwell's deadline for political nightmare, was upon us. In my old wooden Lightning I sailed a last tour along the bright foliage-rimmed sound. Furiously I rode my bike to the post office and back. I tried to concentrate on reading manuscripts for the Editors' Book Award—dozens of overlooked books—and even tried to resurrect Willie Charles, my young pseudonymous alter ego: "Willie Charles will be a crusader for simple justice. A sentimental and direct kid. His reaction to worldwide barbarism will be simple amazement," I scribbled in my journal.

But still Willie Charles himself had not scribbled a word.

And none of this could keep my mind off November 10.

At October's end, I went to a Sunday party in New York, missed the bus home, waited for a train at a bar, and got smashed. I telephoned Annie for help. She met the midnight train, having driven through a rain-plastered night for her totally plastered husband.

The conductor led me down the steps. He had permitted me to ride for fifty-six cents after I blurted out that I had no more money, that my wife was expecting a baby, and we were waiting for the results of an awful, murderous test. For that simple act of pity I have always thanked that nameless conductor.

On November 7, three days before the test result deadline, Annie visited Dr. Livoti and was told again of her baby's mighty heartbeat. She was allowed to begin moderate exercise.

She returned, joking and hopeful.

I remembered the last time we had been confident, our sexual evening, and I worried about the sin of hubris, and the penalties.

On November 9, I was on the verge of panic. Now all my sins would be punished. The baby would be declared a non-human lump because of the father's lusting after two women, and boozing.

I wrote a note to myself that if our baby were defective and murdered, I would flee to a small town in the western desert and drink myself to death. I picked Thompson, Utah, a speck on the map, as my destination.

On the Day, November 10, a Thursday, Annie and I waited by the phone. Nothing.

At noon, I left for my garage and attempted to answer mail. Anxious, overlooked authors wanted to know who had won the Editors' Book Award. At 3:15 P.M., I noted in the journal: "Storm coming, windy, dark, leaves stripped from the trees totally in one afternoon. Still no word of *you*, child."

On Friday there was no call either.

I knew then that the news had to be bad. Dr. Livoti was searching for diplomatic words to describe the horror. Neither of us would call her because while the phone was silent, there was still hope.

During the weekend, we both turned to granite in our sorrow. We were so pessimistic that I resolved to be optimistic just for the heck of it. Somehow, we had to get to Monday when Dr. Livoti returned to her office.

Like both days of the weekend, Monday was cold and gray with not a hint of sun. I fled to the garage to escape the phone at home. Every time it rang, we both lunged to answer, but the caller was never Livoti.

About noon, I worried that Annie, if she received bad news, might collapse and not be able to telephone me.

So I went home.

Because both of us were about to snap, I dared to call Livoti's office and mention that we were waiting for the amniocentesis results and would they call us back and let us know when, just when, we might have the verdict. I didn't want the results, really, just a timetable, I explained, my voice breaking.

I drove to the little country store down the road for Annie's favorite clam chowder, a box of pretzels, and milk and returned in a few minutes.

The phone rang.

"Mr. McCoy?" It was Irene, the nurse.

"Mr. Henderson, Annie's husband."

"Oh, I'm sorry."

"That's OK."

"Do you want to know the sex and everything?"

Then I knew.

Our baby was OK.

"Yes! The sex and everything!"

"It's a wonderful, healthy girl!" Irene shouted with real elation, as if she hadn't announced this to hundreds of parents before me.

I yelled for Annie. I asked Irene to repeat this to Annie directly. Then I held Annie as Irene shouted her happiness, and Annie's eyes glistened for all of us.

At that moment, after days of darkness, sunlight saturated the tiny room. The sun shone for a few minutes while we called friends and Annie's mother and Lady Bea in England. Then it disappeared again for days.

When I was a young boy, the living room where I sat playing with my blocks was once filled with light, and I knew that God had entered that room.

It's hard not to think of God's blessing when the sun shines out of nowhere at a moment like Irene's call. Mere weather fact. A coincidence. I know.

I know.

I laugh at myself. God in the sunshine. A Hallmark card. But I can't forget it. Why at that second? Did the ringing phone rend the clouds asunder? There, that's it. A scientific explanation. The ringing phone did it.

A girl! How perfect, I thought. A mother to children. Somebody I could talk to, like I talked to my mother and seldom to my silent father.

Annie adored women. They were her easy and true pals. Men were from a distant planet, light-years away.

I had a bit more understanding of men than Annie. Most men were rather simple machines, I thought. Good for jobs, football, and war. I remembered my scorn of my Pop, a decent, quiet, shy man, who didn't deserve my anger. Like me, he wanted to witness for the Truth. His shyness chained him. Only booze broke me out of my timidity. We were kin, not competitors.

The world seemed about to be obliterated by male competition. "Missile Envy," author Helen Caldicott called it. The Russians had just broken off arms control talks in Geneva and were trigger-happy. In September they shot down a Korean Airlines plane, killing 271 passengers. It had strayed over their space and was spying, they explained.

Into that sort of era, my child, Holly, was about to be born. The End of Everything hung over us like a constant low-grade fever.

That weekend, friends gave a party to celebrate Holly. Near the end of the party, after several Wild Turkeys, I ran into a *New Yorker* writer, an acquaintance of Jonathan Schell and an essayist specializing in medical mysteries.

"Here's a medical mystery for you," I told him. "How come we are within seconds of obliterating this planet and we go about day to day as if nothing much was happening? Nothing at all! This is sin, you know. The antithesis of Love. You are in sin, I am in sin. We will destroy the world for our children. Did you see the 'Today' show? Adelman and that little girl asking about nuclear accidents? She saw what could happen. A child! And he ignored her! We act as if nothing is going on! Nothing! Sinnnnnn. . ." I proclaimed in his face.

With that, I reeled back into a chair where I sat alone while the party hummed around me. I didn't hear the *New Yorker* writer's reply, or even if he made one.

"Love is God! We sin against Love!" I babbled over and over. Why wasn't my dead pen pal, Ruth Carter, here? She'd get it. Not this thick bunch.

Nobody let on that they noticed me. People often drank too much at these events. They were politely helped out and driven home.

The next day, nobody would mention it.

14

Evangelist

AS ANNIE'S belly swelled, she was bombarded with birthing advice from female strangers. At a dinner party, a fanatic scolded her: Annie had to practice the new ancient Norwegian massage method, much better than Lamaze, which was now strictly passé, and as for modified Lamaze, don't even mention it, growled the woman, angry at Annie for her ignorance.

Annie left the table and hid in the bathroom.

"I'm already a bad mother. I don't even know about the old new Norwegian way," she worried on the drive home.

Dr. Livoti suggested that a modified Lamaze class might be helpful.

At the start of February, we gathered with a group of expectant parents in a fluorescent-lit room in Lenox Hill Hospital. Our tutor was Kathy, a young, perky nurse who worked in the hospital's delivery room. Kathy explained that she had yet to experience childbirth personally, but she had assisted in hundreds of births. Her perkiness was reassuring.

We were by far the oldest of the dozen couples in the group, which included a dental surgeon and his wife, always dressed in a different expensive maternity outfit for each class, and a black girl and her girlfriend, who giggled at Kathy's breathing technique drills and her cheerleading about practicing our exercises at home.

I wanted to hear only about pain and how to get rid of pain.

On the first evening, Kathy asked for a male volunteer. When no man raised his hand, she told me to stand up from my metal folding chair and come forward. "Now, Bill, if you were walking down the street and a stranger came up to you and did this, what would you do?"

Kathy balled up her fist and slammed it into my stomach, softening the blow at the last second.

I bent double in reaction.

"Well, Bill, what would you do?"

"I'd ask them what they wanted?" I tried.

Annie laughed loudly.

Kathy looked at the ceiling.

"No. You would try to avoid the pain by tensing up, just as you did . . . which is wrong," instructed Kathy. "The point of Lamaze is that you go *with* the pain and not against it."

I was sent to my seat.

Going with the pain meant concentrating on regular breathing, timed contractions, and fixation on a focal point.

Next week Kathy unrolled a life-size wall chart of a woman's insides. With a doll in her hand, she explained what would happen on the days before birth. The baby would shift into a head-down position and dilation of the cervix would begin and then contractions and then the baby would begin its journey.

In the next few classes we practiced breathing control and floor muscle exercises—I held Annie's feet for her sit-ups and felt generally left out.

My only job on birth day would be to hold Annie's hand when the hard contractions started, to insist that she breathe rhythmically, to supply her with ice chips for her lips when requested, and to insist that she concentrate on our chosen focal point—a photo of me cradling Sophie as a puppy on a sunny beach.

In the back of my mind, a constant question: When do we hear about the drugs? I was not impressed with Lamaze or any other fad birthing theories about bonding with my wife and child or rhapsodizing about the agony.

I worried about Annie's pain.

I wanted Holly born quickly.

This was not poetry, not a Polaroid opportunity with dad snapping the first bloody sightings for the ogling of friends and relatives. Birth was a practical matter. "What about drugs?" I finally blurted.

Kathy sniffed that we would hear about that in the next-to-last class, and quickly moved on to something else.

Late in February, Kathy guided us on a tour of the new-baby unit. We were issued gowns, inspected the chamber of the newborns, and we peeked into the delivery-room area. Down the hall, a woman wailed nonstop.

I looked at Annie. She looked at me. Kathy shut the door fast.

Kathy eventually got to the drugs as promised. Saddleblock. An epidural. A spinal injection that killed the pain for a few hours but did not interfere with the mother's labor and did no harm to the child. That's what I wanted to hear. A little Natural Childbirth and lots of Saddleblock.

For the final class, only weeks before Holly's scheduled delivery, we were ushered into the Lenox Hill Hospital auditorium for a film about four labors. We watched the four women controlling their breaths and timing their contractions and focusing on their focal points. We admired the husbands holding their hands, dealing out ice chips, and comforting them between tantrums and shrieks and sharing their triumph as the babies squalled out to be wrapped and footprinted.

The film allowed us to examine the final gory close-up of only one birth—the actual detailed, full-screen emergence of the child from the vagina.

I felt reassured. There in the movies was the evidence that all of this was possible. Something so big could make it out of there.

Suddenly Annie jumped up and scrambled from the dark theater, her hand over her mouth. Outside, she stood in the hall, shaking her head and sobbing.

"I can't do that. I won't do that. Will not!"

I hugged her as the others filed out, glancing at us with worried frowns. "She'll be OK," I assured Kathy.

But Annie was adamant. She was not going to do what she had seen in the film. Push all of that out of there.

No way.

In the days before Holly's scheduled arrival, it rained steadily.

Inside our New York room, Annie's womb, quiet for nine months, was suddenly not her own. Holly had gone berserk—squirming, kicking, twisting. Annie could only wait and wonder.

We waited two blocks from Lenox Hill Hospital in a suite at the Hyde Park Hotel, rented for the month of March by Lady Beatrice, in town for Holly's birth. Together we marveled at Annie's tummy turmoil.

In the Lamaze class we had become experts in dilations and contractions, but we knew nothing about infant prebirth misbehavior. So far, Holly gave no signs that she was about to allow herself to be born.

Annie was uncomfortable with her sister and me. For nine months she had controlled her pregnancy and, except for the scares, been content. Now, with two days to go, she was under nattering observation.

Even the local newspaper noticed her journey to New York from Wading River: Her photo was on the front page as she waited for the bus. "Waiting" was the caption.

Now her sister and I clamored at her. "Look at this weather. Aren't we lucky you took my advice and came into the city early, Annie? What if this turned to snow and we had eighty miles of driving?" I commented, congratulating myself on my amazing weather-predicting ability.

Since there was little else to do, we rented a VCR, watched videos, and ate too much.

At noon on March 13, we had dined locally and were on our

way back to the hotel when Annie felt a trickle. She checked herself in the bathroom. "I think my water just broke," she said.

This was the Sign. Since the baby would not live without fluid for long, we had to get to the hospital.

The rain was worse, but we had only a short walk. A technician tested the trickle with litmus paper and declared her water had not broken.

"Of course it has," Annie said. She smeared a sample of the water on her finger and tasted it. "That's not pee."

The technician sighed and tested again, with the same results. We huddled under the umbrella and leaned back into the rain. In Annie's womb, Holly continued to dance, but not as frantically.

For the evening, we rented *Frances*, a movie about the actress Frances Farmer, famous for a brief time and then lobotomized for recurring mental illness.

We stuffed ourselves with takeout Chinese—mushu pork, shrimp with snow peas, fried dumplings. The opened fortune cookies portended nothing special.

Annie herself had been born after a ten-month pregnancy. Perhaps Holly was a month away. Now Holly was quiet.

"I just know my water broke," Annie said.

"He did check twice," I said.

"He could have been wrong twice, and if he was wrong Holly is in trouble."

We sat and worried.

Lady Bea wasn't feeling well. Annie and I blamed the food. "No, I think I have the flu," Bea said.

Outside, the rain was turning to wet snow.

Bea said goodnight and vomited in the bathroom.

About ten o'clock, Annie developed a toothache—a molar next to her wisdom tooth on the upper left side. She took a Tylenol.

I telephoned the front desk and asked if they knew of an emergency dentist on call to the hotel. The guy laughed. "You'll have to wait until morning. Lots of dentists in New York."

"This is Lady Beatrice Ashley's room," I tried. Maybe Bea's title would get him hopping.

"So?"

I lay down next to Annie and held one hand while she held her jaw with the other. In her purse she had discovered some Ambesol. She rubbed that on the molar and it seemed to help.

Depressed and helpless to do anything about her pain, I fell asleep next to her about midnight.

I noticed that the wet snow had increased to what seemed to be a blizzard.

The first contraction hit at 12:35 A.M. It hit hard and it hurt bad.

Annie, clutching her aching mouth, bent over in bed and tried not to scream. Her focal point was still in her suitcase.

I got up to get it. But between the tooth and the contractions, she was not interested in looking at Sophie and me.

"Go with the pain, go with the pain," she coached herself, and tried to follow her breathing instructions. "If this is just the start, I'm not going to finish," she told me.

When the contraction passed, she sat up and waited for the next one. It didn't happen.

Annie got out of bed and went into the next bedroom to tell her sister: "I just had a contraction. A big one."

"I'm so sick," moaned Bea.

Annie swallowed the next-to-last Tylenol and turned on the TV. The talk shows were signing off. The few movies didn't interest her, but on a cable channel she discovered a man with white hair, a white beard, a white suit, and a crazed stare directed at a single camera. He frightened her. So she switched around the dials again.

The tooth's pain was taking her over, mind and body. She was becoming pain.

Nothing on TV distracted her except that mad-looking fellow, Dr. Danny Berke and his "Trumpet of Winged Victory" show. He said his mission was "to save all the jerks of the world."

Here was an evangelist with a twist. Not once did he mention forgiveness or sweetness. He demanded that you get your life together with Jesus or you were a twit.

Dr. Danny was assisted by a miniskirted girl who also seemed to run the single camera. She appeared from behind the camera now and then to hand him notes and newspaper clippings. "Delia just dug out a wowser. Says there's an epidemic of teen suicides. Today's *Times*. The creeps can't even get Jesus's message to the kids! This is entirely unnecessary!"

In the background, on a stark all-white set, a three-piece rock band filled in when Dr. Danny ran out of outbursts. "Up from the Grave He Arose, with a Mighty Victory o'er His Foes," they played.

Dr. Danny sang along, and opened up with his own trumpet from time to time.

This woke me from my semi-doze. "Who's that?" I asked Annie.

"I don't know. I just found him. He seems so sure of himself."

"Is it any better, the tooth? What can I do?"

She shook her head to answer both questions.

I returned to my uselessness.

The evangelist had a caller, a homosexual who wanted to switch to hetero. "A child of Sodom on the line! Listen, kid, haven't you been listening for the last two hours? Get right with Jesus. Stop crapping around! It's simple! Just do it, pervert!" He slammed down the phone, briefly rose in fury from his stool and sat down again to scowl.

The band ripped into a hymn.

There were no commercial breaks on Dr. Danny's "Trumpet of Winged Victory" show. Apparently he had no sponsors. He owned the channel.

I watched with Annie while he plunged on into the night. Danny was her comfort, her white noise. They shared agony in the snow-quiet dark.

"Sunday's not the sabbath! Friday is! They lie to you, the entire goose-gaggle of them! If they lie about Sunday, they lie about everything else!"

His madness became Annie's direction. It was a place to aim the toothache, out there with Dr. Danny.

He was launching into the cocaine sins of John DeLorean, defrocked automaker, when the second major contraction hit. It drove Annie from the TV into the bathroom.

Like Dr. Danny's props, the bathroom too was stark, with old-fashioned white tiles and a white, claw-footed tub.

Annie decided she must wash her hair. She wanted to look right for her doctors. She sat on the edge of the tub and thought about her hair.

There was one more Tylenol. After another contraction, she swallowed it.

She strapped on her wristwatch and began timing the contractions.

"Jezebel! God wants you!" she heard the evangelist screaming at a caller. "Harlot!"

Annie retrieved a half-filled quart bottle of vodka hidden in the bottom of her suitcase. After nine months of abstinence, she downed half a tumbler straight and rested on the toilet seat. "What the hell!" she said, and drank another half-tumbler.

The vodka didn't kill the pain. But it removed it. She floated in space. Now it was just Holly and herself, and the tooth.

She forgot to clock the contractions.

Snow splattered on the windows.

She lay down on the bathroom floor and slept.

⌐15

Tooth

I WOKE at first light.

The evangelist had finally signed off. The empty screen hissed.

Annie sat next to me, trying to see her watch. "The contractions are seven minutes apart," she told me. "I'm all out of Tylenol."

Finally I had something to do. "I'll find a drugstore and be right back. Then we'll call a dentist," I announced, pulling on my pants and jacket.

"At 5:30?" she called after me.

Outside the snow was stopping. A wind iced the wet pavements. Over Queens, the sun had just appeared weakly.

I slipped and slid toward the East River. An early-morning drugstore might be open soon. I'd find the Extra Strength Tylenol and end that pain.

Just down the block, I spotted a bronze plaque, a dentist's office. I memorized his name and the phone number printed under it.

At Seventy-seventh and Third, I turned south and slipped onward. A newsstand was opening. "Gary Hart Wins Big in Massachusetts, Rhode Island and Florida," was headlined. I asked for Tylenol, but he had only aspirin. Three blocks farther, a newsstand had Tylenol, but not Extra Strength. I'd hold out for Extra Strength. I swung over to Second Avenue, headed north.

A few commuters were on the street, migrating south by foot, crowding into the subway entrances. At one subway, a politician was already campaigning, shaking hands and begging for votes. I pushed through the mob and finally discovered an open drugstore. In the window was the entire Tylenol lineup, including Extra Strength.

"Extra Strength Tylenol!" I yelled to the druggist.

He grabbed a box, stuffed it into a bag, and I skidded back to the hotel, ran into the room, and found Annie on the phone talking to a friend, trying to remember the name of a dentist, a mutual pal. From the bag, I produced the box in triumph. But it was not Extra! The druggist had grabbed the wrong box. Just plain Tylenol! I had failed to be useful.

Annie gulped three capsules, without any relief.

The contractions were at six-minute intervals.

I dialed the number of the dentist down the street. His answering machine said he was on vacation and a dentist in midtown would take calls at regular hours.

I telephoned my own dentist at home in Garden City. He said he'd be glad to help at two P.M. when he got into his office on Forty-ninth Street. I said OK. A standby.

Finally Annie remembered the name of her mutual friend, a dentist on Central Park South. It was 7:20. She dialed. A nurse, just arrived, said the dentist had an opening at eleven A.M.

"But I'm having a baby!" Annie cried, as another contraction hit.

I picked up the phone. "Come right in," the nurse told me.

Central Park South was twenty blocks away. It was rush hour.

Annie dressed and we walked down to the sidewalk. Every six minutes a contraction bent her double. We had to stop and wait for her to recover. Cabs filled with rush-hour passengers swarmed by. Not a chance that one would be empty.

In desperation, holding the bent-over Annie, I thrust my hand like a plea to the sky.

An empty cab braked immediately. I had no time to think of answered prayers.

Hoping for a safe and swift ride, I said: "My wife is having a baby," and gave the dentist's address.

At the word *baby,* the driver bolted forward, dodging traffic, throwing us around in the back seat. "Jeez, a baby," he muttered, beating a red light, his eyes on Annie in the rear-view mirror. Not in his cab was she going to have a baby.

At the dentist's building, we waited with the arriving office employees and packed into an elevator for the ride up, hoping that a contraction wouldn't bend Annie over in the jammed box.

The dentist was ready for us. He took a quick look at her molar and pronounced, "It's abscessed and has to come out immediately." But since Annie was in labor, he had to consult about the Novocain. He dialed Dr. Livoti's number.

Carol said there was no way Annie could have Novocain until she checked her out.

We headed for Seventy-ninth and Second, back into the frenzied streets.

On the park side of Central Park South, I spotted a cab pulling up. I fled across four lanes of traffic, was at the curbside door before the passengers were out, and ordered the driver to pick up Annie. "She's got to have a tooth out now!" I shouted.

He U-turned through the four lanes and, amid curses and horn blasts, we picked up Annie who, just at that moment was slammed with another contraction. We roared east and then north up Third.

"It's every cabbie's nightmare," said the driver, who was not fooled by my tooth gambit. "Lots of babies in back seats. Lots more than you think."

Dr. Livoti was not fully awake. At her desk, she regarded a

Styrofoam coffee cup. Instead of her usual Italian greeting, she yawned: "What seems to be happening? Make it interesting."

"My contractions are six minutes apart," Annie said.

"Not interesting." Carol waved her hand in dismissal.

"This tooth."

"Let's have a look." In the next room, she eased Annie back on the examination table and felt her abdomen with her hands. "Oh, God! She's turned on us!" Carol shouted. "Holly's turned herself completely around. Her head's straight up! It's a breech!"

Suddenly our doctor was very awake. "I don't know how to tell you this. Holly was fine ten days ago. Perfectly positioned. But she made up her mind to turn. This is an emergency cesarean. There's no option."

To Annie and me this was fine.

I didn't need the poetry of focal points and ice chips. For Annie, her baby had given her the greatest gift of all: She didn't have to do what she had seen that woman do in the movie and declared she would never, ever do. No way.

"OK," we said.

Carol dialed the dentist. "Get that tooth out quick. Novocain. Anything. I want her back at Lenox Hill immediately!" She banged the desktop with her open hand.

It was past nine A.M., and rush hour had let up. This taxi didn't have to dodge traffic back to the dentist. Annie started to wail: "I'm not an old woman! I don't want to lose my tooth!"

"Hey, lady, it's nothing!" The driver tried to console her.

"It's a terrible, terrible pain!" Annie argued.

"Lady, I had a tooth pulled once and it didn't hurt at all. Seems like it should, with those roots deep in and all, but it don't. Zip and it's out!" he assured her.

This time, it was the dentist who worried about a baby born inconveniently. He hustled her into his chair and injected her gum with Novocain. He impatiently prodded her gum. "Feel that?"

She did. "Do you have to take out my tooth? I've never lost a tooth."

"I tell you: Once in dental school a girl had a baby in my station wagon. Not a lot of laughs." He poked her gum again. "Feel that?"

She didn't. The tooth was yanked and, as the cabbie promised, it was no big deal.

"Can I see my tooth one more time?" Annie asked.

"You sure you want to? It's not pretty." He displayed the bloody tooth. "Want me to wrap it up for you?" Annie let the tooth go.

In the fourth taxi of the morning, Annie lost it. When I told the driver, "Lenox Hill Hospital emergency room," she said, "Hyde Park Hotel. I need to talk with my sister."

"You can't go for a chat now!"

"Hyde Park Hotel," she insisted.

In the middle of Central Park, the driver pulled over. He turned and looked me in the eye. "What's it gonna be, buddy? I haven't got all day and neither does she."

We waited. Annie considered. The driver tapped the dashboard.

"OK, Lenox Hill," Annie whispered.

I told the driver.

"Things are moving too fast," she said. "This used to be *my* baby."

At the hospital, a wheelchair was waiting for her. With no formalities beyond our signatures on a piece of paper, we were dispatched upstairs to the maternity wing. Annie was dressed in a hospital gown and stretched out on a gurney to wait for the anesthesiologist, who was rushing to her side from somewhere.

This was our first quiet moment since dawn. "Holly and I used to be in control. Now everybody else is," Annie said.

After another major contraction, I realized we had forgotten the focal point. We tried a few breathing exercises. Helpless again, I could only hold her hand.

She was starting to shake all over. "I'm sorry. I can't stop it," Annie apologized.

The anesthesiologist hustled in, asked her questions: Was she allergic to penicillin for the tooth abscess infection? What about reactions to anesthesia for her previous ovary operation? He told me, "My wife had a cesarean once. You forget the pain afterward. There's so much happiness you never even notice it."

A nurse followed with an IV bottle and tubes. She punctured Annie's right arm.

I pinched Annie's big toes and kept on pinching hard, hoping to distract her from the pain of the needle. It did no good.

Then it was time to go. We kissed, her lips puffy from the extraction.

They rolled her away to the operating room.

As instructed, I sat alone in a small room decorated with pastel blue wallpaper. At 2:09 P.M., I remembered our standby dentist appointment. When I called to apologize for not showing up and explained why, he was miffed.

I returned to the pastel waiting room, my mind empty. I wasn't afraid or frantic. I didn't pace. I hunched over, alone, stunned. A hunk of stone.

A few feet away, Annie told me afterward, they stood around her body, a staff of six people, including Carol Livoti, in silence.

Annie was told to roll on her side and grab her knees to her chin. "Very hard to do with a pregnant belly," Annie recalled.

They held her like that and stuck a needle into her spine. The epidural.

They rigged up a green tent over her middle to shield the sight of what they were about to do. Carol tapped a toe, double-checking about the drug.

Annie said she felt nothing.

Carol and the others raised their hands over their heads, as if in supplication. "Ready?" she asked them.

"Excuse me," Annie said, and threw up in a bowl by her head, placed there for that purpose.

"Ah, Chinese last night!" noted Carol.

Annie nodded, smiled.

"Let's go." Carol began to cut.

She talked her way into Annie's insides.

"We are entering right above that adorable apple tattoo. Some day you will have to tell us about the night you got that tattoo," Carol joked. "We are right on top of that bikini-line scar from the other operation. That way you won't have two scars . . . very clean inside here . . . very clean! What a beautiful uterus, Annie! Clean as a whistle!"

She cut a bit more, moving quickly.

"There she is! I see Holly! I see her! I've got my hands on her! Just a minute. Just a minute. Oh, she's beautiful! She's beautiful!"

It was 2:32 P.M.

And Holly was lifted into the light.

III

Ellsworth, 1991

—∘*16*

Holly

HOLLY WAS SERENE.

Her dad, who had never held an infant, was terrified he would drop her.

I expected Holly would be wailing after the day's frenzy, but now she smiled slightly. Smiling about what? I asked myself in the recovery room. About her trick of breeching so Annie could keep her pledge not to duplicate the movie mom's agony?

Wondering at her face and eyes that now and then opened and drowsily shut again, I, like trillions of dads before me, simply worshiped my daughter. In her minuscule fingers, perfectly formed, I sensed divinity. How could such perfection be created from such a ridiculous pair of parents? Holly was palpable evidence of something greater than us.

In Holly's face I hunted for clues about her future. Did she resemble my mom, to whom she had been pledged? My shy pop? Annie's sad mother? Would she be like any of them? So far for you to go, Holly, I thought, so far.

Finally, as the stapled-up Annie was wheeled in to caress her child, smiling through puffy lips, I worried: Will Holly like me?

I was astonished by the question. Like her dad?

I had become a boy again, desperate for the praise of women, once again huddled next to my dying mother's bed, waving my latest review in her eyes. As I cradled my daughter, I struggled to still the terrors in my mad male heart.

Holly was calm about all that, as calm as my mother had been.

After reading this memoir, Annie suggested that I add a chapter about Holly now, almost eleven years later—about Holly's grace, beauty, humor, kindness.

But Holly's story is hers to tell some day, if she wishes. Perhaps like my mother, she will see no importance in notes on paper. Perhaps Holly's lived life will be a sufficient record for her.

Some scattered snapshots perhaps, in no particular chronological order.

From the start, Holly took over our lives, and her own. I thought I would be busy nurturing her, an important fellow. But she fed at Annie's breast, slept most of the time in her profound calm, and grew strong. Aside from diaper duty now and then, I wasn't essential. If it weren't for Holly's welcoming smile, I might have felt useless.

Holly didn't just smile; she grinned in an open-mouthed *gaaaa* of hilarity. If she were sitting up, she'd often blast herself over backward with her *gaaaa* and lie in her bassinet flapping her arms like a tiny bird. She couldn't get enough of her visitors. She looked hard at them, concentrating on their faces, studying them.

I wanted to talk with her, to know who she was, what she knew. I couldn't wait for her words.

When I had held the glass to my dying mother's lips, I felt so close, but so far away. What was it like to be dying? I had wanted to become my mother's mind.

Now, as I held a bottle to Holly's lips, I longed to know what it was like to be just born, to be so excited that almost any event set her to slapping both her knees in delight.

By the end of November, Holly was crawling about her

playpen and standing by holding onto the bars. Annie and I noticed that when the radio was on Holly swayed to the music.

Holly was beginning to dance.

For months she stood in place, supported by her parents, bobbing and bouncing, clapping her hands, interpreting any rhythm available. When, with excited giggles, she walked alone for the first time, it was more an extension of her dancing than a new skill.

She seldom merely walked—she either ran or danced. She learned how to put a tape in the stereo and Annie and I would wake to her music from the living room downstairs, soon named "The Dance Room" by Holly. There she danced in front of a floor-to-ceiling mirror, perhaps imitating the bouncing ladies at Annie's exercise class.

Holly wasn't particular about her music—Beach Boys, Rolling Stones, or *Oklahoma!* were OK with her. But Gershwin's *Rhapsody in Blue* was her favorite. Usually naked, she interpreted Gershwin's nuances in precise coordination with arms, legs, head, her whole body, bounding and bowing with rolls and somersaults, slow, fast, graceful, manic, and always with an inspiration that knew no design or choreographer.

With dance she made peace. If Annie was moody or Daddy was fussy, Holly snagged us and pulled us into her dance room, where she insisted that we twirl and jump with her. She led, we followed. She was no easy instructor, and there was never any excuse for not dancing. Holly hounded her reluctant parents from room to room. "Dance! Dance, now!"—until we gave in and spun to her lead. I, who hadn't danced for years, now stooped to encircle her waist and learn all over again the lessons of rhythm.

Only once had I danced like Holly. Drunk, on a restaurant table, a college sophomore, I pranced and was glorious. I ate the flowered centerpiece. For Holly, no booze was required, and it wasn't necessary to eat the flowers.

Summer evenings we took the radio to a bay beach and Holly danced with us or by herself in the sunset. When the moon rose she practiced the sound of her new word, *moooooooon*. She called out, reaching for it.

On winter evenings, Holly staged her own performances for us. Annie, drama major and TV veteran, strung a sheet across the dance room and dimmed the lights. "Presenting Holly Henderson!" she called and we applauded as Holly entered, bottomless or in her pink tutu, from behind the sheet, bowing and waving into my flashlight beam. Holly liked the entrance almost as much as the dance and she'd return behind the sheet and reappear over and over until Annie coached, "It might be time for the show now, Holly." Then Holly was gone into *Rhapsody in Blue*, the entire two sides of the tape and asking to start over.

How did she know all of this? I am reminded of Wordsworth, ". . . trailing clouds of glory do we come/From God . . ." Annie remembered a friend who listened on the house extension as her four-year-old asked the infant in its crib upstairs, "Tell me about God. I'm beginning to forget."

Holly taught me again how to kiss. Her kiss asked for nothing, withheld no information, was given without reservation. It had no history, no future, wanted only the moment.

Because Holly's kisses carried no baggage, she soothed her granny's last years. When she and Annie flew south, Holly ran helter-skelter to her granny's wheelchair with greetings that knew nothing of her drinking or past agony.

When news came that Granny had died, Holly's kisses comforted Annie while my kisses could offer only reserved sympathies.

Holly was always mannerly. "Dank do," she'd say when given her bottle. "Bite?" "Sip?" she'd ask, wanting to share. "Hi you! Comere. Sit der," she'd greet a visitor to her play table.

"Hurt? Hurt?" she worried, touching the shin I'd just banged, or Annie's scalded finger, or Sophie's stepped-on tail. In her question was the healing prayer.

Once when I lay on the sofa with fever, she constructed an elaborate ceremony for me on the rug with a jump rope, a chunk of chalk, her mittens, and a magic song. It worked. In the morning I was better.

When we passed a flattened rabbit on the road one Easter morning, I quipped, "Looks like the Easter bunny didn't make it this year."

She was on me immediately. "Not funny, Daddy."

"Sorry," I apologized to my indignant five-year-old. We rode in silence.

"I wonder how it happened?" Holly asked, noticing my sulking.

I shook my head.

"Not that you were there, Daddy," she added, freeing me from road-kill complicity. Later she admitted she never thought it was the *real* Easter bunny. In fact, she hadn't believed in that bunny, or in Santa Claus either. "You and Mom wanted me to believe, so I pretended to. I didn't want to hurt your feelings."

I worried about Holly's empathy for squashed bunnies, banged shins, scalded fingers, and stepped-on tails. I worried even more about the onslaught of erect boys that was only a few years away. She might be too tender for a world where kindness was a luxury.

Then I remembered the incident of the plastic scooter. Holly was about three. The scooter was bigger than she was and weighed more, too. She wanted to drag it into the house but she couldn't fit it through the sliding glass door. A wheel caught, or the handlebars. From the corner of the yard I watched her. Only a week before, she would have called for Daddy's help. But this matter was between herself, the scooter, and the door. She yanked, she twisted, she flipped that scooter, and she didn't complain. Some way the scooter was going in. Finally, she kicked it and it clattered into the house.

I saw that there was a core of Holly that was not to be messed with, by scooter or human.

One day that same year she learned the importance of her name.

"Hey, kid!" I called as she dashed across the yard.

She stopped, hands on hips. "Name's Holly!" she yelled.

"OK, OK, Holly," I agreed, and never called her "kid" again lightly.

Soon the "Holly" was joined to a last name. "Name's Holly Hunnerson," she told guests as she considered them eye to eye.

And there was even more for her to be proud about two months later.

"Guess what, Daddy."

"I give up. What?"

"I'm a girl!" she shouted.

This was real news and she knew it immediately. Huge news. Holly. Holly Hunnerson. A girl!

And tough enough to kick a scooter through a door without apologies.

Holly, like her mom, loved a joke. Any joke.

One afternoon, at our Maine summer house, she snuck up the steps to the loft where I was napping over a manuscript and pounced on me, sitting on my chest.

"Daddy, say after me."

"OK."

"Watta."

"Watta."

"Goose."

"Goose."

"Siam."

"Siam."

"What a goose I am, you said that." And she ran downstairs to tell Annie about her marvelous trick on Dad.

Her humor was far more scatological than I had been permitted as a boy. One morning we all lay in the summer predawn darkness and heard a bird begin to sing. The bird was creating an elaborate song, really working out, when he seemed to notice that he was all alone. The bird shut up and sang no more.

"Holly," I said, "that bird got up too early. He made a dope of himself. Now he's sitting out there in the dark all embarrassed and red-faced."

Holly hooted. And farted under the covers. Because of the fart, she hooted again. And farted again. She ran out of the room hooting and farting and hooting at the red-faced bird and her own embarrassment.

One morning in Wading River, Holly woke me quite early. "Daddy, come quick. It's 'mazing."

I didn't want to wake, but she whispered in my ear over and over, "It's 'mazing." She led her grumpy dad to her room.

A huge full moon was setting in the west and through another window the sun, even larger, was rising from the direction of the ocean at our backs.

I sat on her bed and shared her rapture.

Every year our little village put on a Halloween party for the children. When Holly was six, the minister's wife, dressed as a Gypsy fortuneteller, set up headquarters in a tent in the local hall. Holly, dressed as a little witch with green hair and a hearthside broom, entered the tent to have her palm read by the mysterious lady. The tent door flapped shut behind her, and the future was revealed to her.

Suddenly Holly plunged back out through the flap, losing her hat, shouting and running, her palms held out before her. "Mommy, Mommy, I'm so 'cited! The lady told me I'll have three babies when I grow up!"

She stared at the wonder in her hands and for a long time would not close them.

Holly sat on the toilet, thinking, while I shaved. "Sometimes I wonder what it's like to be another person."

"I wonder about that, too," I said. "I wonder what it's like to be you, Holly."

"What's it like to be you, Daddy?"

I put my razor down. Looking at her in the mirror, I attempted. "Well, most days I work at Pushcart Press in the garage. I make phone calls. Think up ideas for books. Write in my journal. Pack books in boxes."

"Oh," she said, reaching for the toilet paper.

"That's a very good question you asked, Holly."

Holly looked at me, flushed the toilet, and left without comment, perhaps already on to the next wonder, perhaps disappointed by my lame answer.

One August night on our Maine summer island, Annie, Holly, and I drove to a hilltop cemetery to watch the annual Perseid shooting star showers. We lay on the blanket and stared upward together into the clear, cold sky.

It wasn't a great night for shooting stars, but the crickets were berserk with song.

"Sometimes I hear crickets sing and sing and then I sleep and they stop. I wake up because I can't hear them anymore. It's so quiet I wonder what happened to them," Holly commented.

We listened some more. "How do crickets sing, Dad?"

"Well, they rub their legs together . . ."

"But how does that make music?"

Long ago I had wondered about that too. But time had passed and I forgot to wonder, just as time rushed over the people buried in this cemetery and over the three of us sitting on this hillside watching for brief, sudden passages of light.

"I don't know," I said.

Simple wonders. The Blue Hill Fair. Home of Wilbur the pig and Charlotte and her web. A warm, windy Maine day. Holly and her friend Ellie sampling fried dough and cotton candy. Sheepdog trials and oxen pulls and bagpipers. And two lop-eared baby rabbits that Holly and Ellie adopted. And that twirling merry-go-round, Holly on a striped zebra, Ellie on a spotted giraffe. Protective parents standing next to them. Annie and her video camera outside the rail attempting to capture the moment. Holly and Ellie in timeless, whirling laughter as a giant pipe organ kept the beat.

"Dad, what will people say we did?" Holly asked me one afternoon as we were driving to the dentist for our checkups. Her class had just visited the town marine museum and its farming and fishing artifacts.

I had no answer. One hundred years from now what would we have left behind? "They'll say we drove cars, had children, lived in houses, got our teeth checked . . ."

"No. What will they say we *did*?"

"You know what it's called when you think about the past, Holly? 'N-o-s-t-a-l-g-i-a.'" I spelled it out for her. A new word, ducking the question. "Nostalgia is when you remember things. Like I remember you as a baby, still needing to get your diapers changed."

"Dad!" Holly scolded.

I shut up.

The dentist said our teeth were fine. But afterward, her question wouldn't leave me. Farm, fish? No, I decided: We bought stuff and sold stuff, that was the answer. All was for sale, all we cared about. Sex and Love sold best. Would we leave behind plows and fishing gear? No. Only stuff—and lots of electronic gizmos.

People might note our busy lifestyle—a style that seemed to change from month to month, but a busyness that never changed as we rushed from place to place and fired off empty electronic messages.

Holly, I could have said, they might say we did nothing at all.

Holly resisted math, just as I had. Her teacher warned us that she was falling behind. Holly attended special classes after school to help her.

I told Holly that only her teachers needed help, not her. "Haven't I known you for seven years? How long have they known you? Two months?"

Holly complained and cried about math and, as my mother was for me, I was her tutor. We got through it and she made the honor roll.

"Just remember, Holly, I'm your best pal," I said.

"No, you're not. You are my Daddy."

Right again.

Adults made you sit through boring dinners and wouldn't let you eat Spaghettios. Annie insisted on combed hair and neat clothes. Daddy was a fanatic about brushing teeth. One night it all became too much and Holly kicked her foot against the wall, smashing clear through the wallboard. She hadn't known she was that strong and ran off to hide in a closet upstairs, terrified. "Gosh, you're strong," I said, comforting her and coaxing her out.

Another night she fled the adults into a rainy night, screaming, "I hate you, I hate you both and I always will . . . but I still love you."

Foot through the wall, screams in the rain. Even Holly at her worst was sensual.

Until Holly was born I didn't realize what true sensual joy was—watching your child grow up, and learning from her again how to dance, and kiss, and make magic, and to feel sorrow about road-killed rabbits and laugh at silly jokes and fall into rapture about the setting moon and rising sun, and marvel at the mystery that might be hidden in your palm, and wonder about how crickets sing, and strut with pride at your sex and your very own name.

And above all to be constantly and forever amazed.

A few years ago, Annie, Holly, and I sailed to England on borrowed funds to celebrate Annie's fiftieth birthday. We visited Lady Beatrice in her half-crumbled castle and then boated to France for a reunion with Tad and Terry, my friends from my great American novelist days. For them I had so long ago sprouted my Bill Faulkner fertility mustache. They are now the parents of two grown children, thanks to their persistence and their doctor's skill, and no credit to my mustache.

We were walking back to our hotel in the Paris summer twilight. For some reason—a travel tiff—Annie and I were not speaking to each other. I stalked down one side of the sidewalk, Annie the other.

Holly took my hand in hers. She tugged me over to Annie. She placed her free hand in Annie's. Reconciled by Holly's hands, we three walked this way in the dusk, united by unambiguous caring.

This winter afternoon in 1995, as I type the final draft of this confession, Holly and Annie are in the dance room deconstructing the Christmas tree so we can plant it outside. Today at lunch, Holly and I ate slices of pizza and pondered what-ifs. . . . What if I had stayed married to the ex-nun? What if Annie and I had never met at the *Whistle* party? Holly and I couldn't imagine not sitting across from each other at Pizza and Things. Our lives began in wonder and continued in wonder.

After Holly was born, I expected the vast changes that other parents had described. But life resumed a dailiness. Galleys to proof. Review copies to ship with related propaganda. Jacket copy to write. Sales conference exhortations to deliver. Meanwhile, Holly, the infant, slept almost all the time.

Above my desk a reminder was posted: "Love is God." But I seldom looked up. It had been tacked there years before.

Depression was always just on the other side of the mirror. Annie could still reduce me to dust with her tongue. "We have an invisible divorce!" she had yelled once as I was leaving for a sales conference in New York. She was sick of living on next to no income because of my obsession with righteous literature. Her inheritance had dwindled to a few hundred dollars and we were dining most nights on noodles and tuna fish. Our backyard looked like a used-car lot for ancient Volvos. In March the heating oil company had refused to deliver because of unpaid bills and our furnace shut down.

That night, having survived the sales conference on manic energy, I had found myself drinking with a black homeless man on steps inside Grand Central Station. "Life ain't shit," he had counseled me as we shared my pint of apricot brandy between us. The day before I might have passed this guy and silently condemned him for not rising up and finding hard work, but at that moment I had thought he was terrifically profound.

I seriously contemplated taking the next train to Montreal and leaving forever.

The next day, shocked at my depression, I asked myself why I thought that depravity was only in the TV news reports of daily rapes and murders, or in the *New York Times* accounts of 40,000 child deaths *every day* from malnutrition and disease caused for the most part by corruption, greed, and stupidity. Depravity wasn't only out there. It was just the other side of my mirror.

Even the strongest men are brittle creatures, filled with swagger but hardly containing their quiet, constant panic. Soon after my Grand Central collapse, I read Henri Troyat's biography of Tolstoy and I cried uncontrollably at Tolstoy's final flight from his wife to death in a remote country train station. Such a titanic and ridiculous holy fool. Not since my father's death had I lost it like that.

Inside me, some person was desperate to emerge. I lay on the floor sobbing for Tolstoy while Sophie licked my face and the winter sun set. Upstairs Holly slept her Buddha nap.

Love is a word that only children say truly, and only love can forgive as I tried to forgive myself for my Montreal plan. For the rest of us, love is corrupted every day by a cynical culture and our own never-ending qualifications.

To Holly, love was as real as a rock. Her "I love you, Momma, Poppa, Sophie" before sleeping was offered without reservations, like her kiss.

At night, after I read her a bedtime story, I'd see her drifting off to sleep and I didn't want her to leave.

"You're a great kid, kid," I said.

"You're a great dad, Dad," she said, curling up.

Please don't sleep, Holly, I whispered to myself. We have so few days together. Don't go to that other place. Stay with me a few minutes more.

Once, lying on the floor by her bed, I dreamed that she was on a subway train in a slum and I couldn't find out what train, or where the train was taking her through the night. I woke up yelling in terror with Annie shaking me.

Now and then I'd stare at Holly in wonder. Her gentle face, her grace. Obviously God was a woman, I'd imagine.

Then I'd wonder at my wonder. Why didn't I spend every moment in amazement at her—at everybody? How could the life of a child, or any life, become ordinary? Another drive to the nursery school, another snapping in of a kid's video on the VCR, another evening meal? How could I allow any second to be routine?

To Holly, no day was ordinary, no love ever undemonstrated.

Once, Holly and I forgot to take her lunch with us to Judy's Play School. A half hour after I dropped her off with our usual hugs and kisses, I reappeared with the Big Bird lunch box.

"Holly, look who's here!" Judy called across her backyard to Holly on the swing.

"Daddy!" Holly screamed, scrambling off the swing and running breakneck across the yard to crash into my arms.

"We forgot your lunch, Holly," I managed.

"I love my daddy."

"There's nothing like it, is there?" said Judy.

I could only nod and hug Holly back in her never-quit hug.

With Holly's friends, affection was never muted. They didn't need a boozy cocktail party or a church moment of peace to inspire a kiss. Their love for each other was a matter of every moment. To walk down the street holding hands or with their arms around each other wasn't a bit remarkable. Love was the way it was for them; the moon, the stars, everything.

Love was not a matter of glancing up at a yellowing quote tacked to the wall.

In Maine a few summers ago, I'd had a rough day: In the mail, lousy reviews for a recent Pushcart title and an agent's crabby letter rejecting an early version of this memoir. "I kept waiting for Bill to grow up," she said, not buying my hope that if I told the truth from my heart it would reach others.

I stood alone on a rock, looking out to sea. Nearby, Holly piled up a sandcastle using a clamshell for a shovel. She glanced up, saw my face, dropped her shell, and walked over to me. Silently she leaned against my leg, watching the sea, a quiet support.

"Try not to worry, Dad."

"OK, Holly. I'll only worry about you."

"I love you, Daddy."

"That's good to know."

"But you already know that!" she scolded, astonished that I could have forgotten. And angry.

"You're right. I'm sorry," I said, feeling very stupid.

Later that day we canoed on Lily Pond and I tried to tell Holly about writing this memoir, about the account of the life and death of my mother that begins it, but I choked up and couldn't continue. I pretended to be interested in a beaver dam across the pond. We paddled toward it.

"Did Grandma Henderson know me before she died?" she asked.

"No. But I told her I was hoping you would be born some day. She would have loved you."

We sat in the canoe for a while, waiting for beavers in the still pond.

Patient, caring, a teacher—my mother was like Holly. In 1942, my father had constructed a record-maker in the basement and recorded my mother and himself putting their kids to bed.

One night Annie and I listened to that scratchy record and

then we watched Annie's videotape of us—doing the same thing. The children's voices, the adult responses, were almost identical. Is this what Jesus meant by immortality? What's done with love endures? I remember my mother's calls upstairs to see if I was OK; I hear the evening bird song, see the quiet twilight.

Holly completed the circle that began with her. This is a story I found, did not create.

When Holly was very young, I tried to tell her about Christmas. I said it was a birthday party for a kind man named Jesus who lived long ago and said the most important rule of all was that we love God and love each other just as much as we love ourselves. I stumbled on that word *love*, had to dig my nails into my palms.

Holly looked at me brightly. "Jesus needs a birthday present. How about a Mr. Potato Head?"

Last year, when Holly had long since grown bored with Mr. Potato Head and had only recently lost interest in Sunday school, she read the *New York Times* over my shoulder and commented about a news horror, "I think it's most important of all that people should love each other and not being good to another person is bad."

"Holly," I said, "you know all you will ever need to know."

Annie took Holly to Sunday school after she heard a friend's tale: The friend had gone to church with her sixteen-year-old daughter for the first time and the daughter thought it was all hilarious. She laughed out loud during the service.

Annie appreciated tradition. To her, church was ceremonies, songs, pageantry, and Sunday outfits. She wanted Holly to know these traditions and not think they were comic. So she dressed her up and enrolled her in the Sunday school of the tiny village Presbyterian church, no bigger than a storefront with an old steeple that slanted toward the rear as if about to crash down on the congregation.

"Where's Mr. Henderson?" the Irish minister asked at the coffee hour. "That's a good Presbyterian name."

But I was having none of his church. The idea of walking through a church door after decades of absence, except for ceremonies, evoked astonishing dread. Perhaps I thought I'd meet my father there. I'd have to deal all over again with his shyness and silence. I had contempt for church doctrine and all who believed such tales. How brain-dead they seemed! Miracles! The Son of God! The Resurrection! Had they ever once thought about any of it? How annoying—and horrifying—that they might welcome me back with their Christian grins.

On the night of February 25, 1990, our part of Long Island was entombed by a record blizzard. Not much moved on Sunday morning and the town's plows managed to cut only a narrow lane to the village center past the church.

My usual Sunday morning ritual was common: a bagel and coffee in bed with the *New York Times*. But outside I could see no *Times* delivered on the mounds of snow that were increasing by the minute.

"We're off to church!" Annie announced through the door to the bathroom, where I sat on the toilet contemplating a *Times*less morning.

"You can't drive down there!" I yelled through the door.

"Yes, I can!" she called back.

In seconds I reasoned that I had to get hold of a *Times* to survive the morning in good habit and that I could also chauffeur Holly and Annie safely to church. I'd buy a *Times* at the general store, read it there, and pick them up after services.

But why not go into the church too?

A Zen monk once admitted that he received several enlightenments while evacuating of a morning. Doing the same, I pondered why I was so afraid of church. Hadn't I once jumped naked into a pile of fornicating people and thought it seemed like church? I hadn't feared that. Why now? Coward.

"I'm coming too!" I hollered to Annie.

I pulled up my pants, found a tie, and we spun off into the blizzard.

The windshield wipers were frozen down. I couldn't free them. I did manage to clear a spot in the windshield but the wet snow quickly covered it. So I drove like a train engineer with my head out the window, very slowly, wiping my eyes with a handkerchief Annie handed me.

With Holly and Annie, I walked through the church door into a mostly empty room. Sunday school was canceled. The organist was snowed in and only a dozen people who lived nearby had turned out. The minister with his Santa Claus white beard carried us in song without the organ. Simple, tentative voices. I heard quiet people trying to carry a tune about a Lord who they hoped would save them somehow from private pain, dread, sorrow, confusion.

During the service, I was singled out by the minister as the stranger in the group and, as was the custom there, asked to explain who I was and how I came to be there.

I stood next to Holly and Annie and said, "I attended a Philadelphia Presbyterian church a long time ago. Today I got here with my head out the car window because the windshield wipers were stuck and I couldn't see the road."

The people laughed.

What happened next is still happening. Since I was a boy I had longed for somebody to talk to me about the church, as my worshiping but silent father had been unable to do. The Irish minister loved to talk almost as much as he loved Jesus. The Bishop of Blarney, I nicknamed him. We became friends.

The man said Holly's word *love* in sermons. He and his congregation sang that word. They promised they loved each other and God. Holly's word seemed real to them, too, as real as a rock. And with that word I imagined they honored the other words that follow from it: awe, wonder, mystery, joy. Holly's other virtues.

Strange words in a poisoned world.

These people confessed that they were like little children.

I saw them as revolutionaries.

Such were my dreams. Of course, later I would discover that they were no better and no worse than any group. Sin was here too, but at least they recognized that word.

The next week the Sunday *Times,* which had been there all along, emerged from the melting drift. The front page headlined "The Universe Is Strangely Ordered, Scientists Find." Holly and I built a huge snow fort from the drift with a front and back door, windows, and a roof so high you could sit up inside.

Friends worried that in my affection for the church I only longed for my past. Not nostalgia, I said. My very soul, hidden for years. Every person's soul, for that matter.

Here at last was my answer to Holly's question: "What's it like to be you, Dad?"

Annie was horrified that I would hit the streets and pass out born-again pamphlets, or start yapping in tongues. To tease her, I began introducing myself at dinner parties as a Christian, a shocking term to our friends, a breach of common sense, and yet another dent in our battered, antique, and therefore priceless, marriage.

"Christians lose themselves in imagination. They adore their stories. They make fools of themselves for love. They say everybody at this table is sacred. Where else do you find that in this society? At your job? At the pub? At the A&P?"

I enjoyed my rebel stance.

"Who was Jesus?" a skeptic asked.

Long gone into history and obliterated by the organized church and political outrages, I admitted.

But Jesus said those words, Holly's words, out loud and simply. Since he died we have been constructing his cathedral, each generation adding a wing, or tearing down an old one. And we crucify him over and over, and resurrect him constantly.

When I joined the church again in November 1990, Annie and Holly heard me lie a bit: "I accept Jesus as my personal savior," I promised the congregation. But I crossed my fingers behind my back and substituted "Love" for "Jesus." Only love saves anybody.

I sinned.

In Maine, I built our house with my bare hands. No power tools at all, I liked to brag. Just a hammer, handsaw, and a T-square. Holly called the old well on the property a "whale," so we named it the Holly Whale House. I was too impatient in 1991 to install Sheetrock interior walls at the Whale House. I resisted the idea of taping and sanding Sheetrock to a fussy finish, so I nailed up real pine paneling. Manly country stuff.

It was on this paneling that Holly banged her head with an awful wallop while bouncing on her bed. Days later she complained suddenly of an excruciating headache and we rushed her to the Island Medical Clinic where the doctor tested her reflexes, flashed lights in her eyes, and advised us to get an immediate CAT scan at the Ellsworth Hospital.

Annie and I placed her on the back seat. I was certain that at any moment Holly would die from a blood clot as we sped north over narrow, blind-crested country roads to the hospital an hour north.

· I swore to myself if Holly died I would kill myself. There was no other reason to live. I'd take my chances on finding her again in the afterlife. By night, I too would be dead.

Later, Annie told me she had planned the same for herself.

Then Grace descended.

This was a word I had never thought about before. Grace. I had never experienced it, couldn't even define it.

Grace.

From nowhere, unsought, and inappropriately. My child was dying. I was doing eighty miles an hour. And this thing happened.

I suddenly felt an enveloping love for the entire universe. Not just for my suffering child. For Annie. For all of it. For all our living and dying.

And I knew I was loved in return. From the very depth of the stars, I was loved.

There would be no suicide, no matter what happened to Holly.

After the CAT scan, the doctor said Holly was OK, and Annie and I collapsed in relief. But in that time I learned a new word.

And Love became palpable.

Love had transcended Holly and Annie and me and infused every pebble on the road as we tore desperately toward Ellsworth.